Industrial Revolution Primary Sources

Industrial Revolution
Primary Sources

James L. Outman
Elisabeth M. Outman

Matthew May, Editor

U·X·L®

THOMSON

★

GALE

Detroit • New York • San Diego • San Francisco • Cleveland • New Haven, Conn. • Waterville, Maine • London • Munich

THOMSON
™
GALE

Industrial Revolution: Primary Sources

James L. Outman and Elisabeth M. Outman

Project Editor
Matthew May

Permissions
Margaret Chamberlain

Imaging and Multimedia
Robert Duncan, Lezlie Light

Product Design
Pamela A. E. Galbreath, Michelle DiMercurio

Composition
Evi Seoud

Manufacturing
Rita Wimberley

LIBRARY OF CONGRESS CATALOGING-IN-PUBLICATION DATA

Outman, James L., 1946–

Industrial Revolution. Primary sources / James L. Outman and Elisabeth M. Outman.

v. cm.

Includes bibliographical references and index.

ISBN 0-7876-6515-0 (hardcover : alk. paper)

1. Industrial revolution—Sources—Juvenile literature. 2. Industrial revolution—Sources. [1. Industrial revolution—Sources.] I. Outman, Elisabeth M., 1951– II. Title.

HD2329 .O98 2003
330.9'034–dc21

2002155420

Printed in the United States of America
10 9 8 7 6 5 4 3 2 1

Contents

Reader's Guide

The Industrial Revolution, which began in England in the middle of the eighteenth century and spread across the globe by the beginning of World War II, shaped a new world. The introduction of new technology into manufacturing processes at the heart of the revolution turned simple agricultural societies into complex industrial ones. Consequently, the way we worked, where we lived, and how we communicated with one another were altered. Governments, even the physical environment of the planet, were forever changed. The Industrial Revolution was in every sense a revolution.

Industrial Revolution: Primary Sources presents twenty-seven full or excerpted written works, speeches, and testimony from the period that provide insight into the thoughts and ideas of some of the era's most important minds. The volume includes excerpts from *An Inquiry into the Nature and Causes of the Wealth of Nations* by Adam Smith, *The Communist Manifesto* of Karl Marx, *Twenty Years at Hull-House* by Jane Addams, and the United States Supreme Court decision in *Northern Securities Co.* v. *United States* enforcing federal regulation of corporations.

Primary Sources is divided into four sections: Economic Theory, Technological Advances and Criticisms, Working Conditions, and Politics and Law. Each document features an introduction, things to remember while reading the excerpt, a glossary of difficult terms from the document, information on what happened after the work was published, and other interesting facts. The volume also includes forty photographs, sources for further reading, a timeline, and an index providing easy access to the subjects discussed throughout *Industrial Revolution: Primary Sources*.

Related reference sources

Industrial Revolution: Almanac, in eight chapters, provides an overview of this era, from its roots in the philosophies of the Renaissance to the first technological advances, from the first migrations of workers to urban areas to the rise of giant corporations. The volume includes nearly sixty photographs, sources for further study, a timeline, a glossary, and an index.

Industrial Revolution: Biographies profiles twenty-five significant figures of the Industrial Revolution. The essays cover such people as economic philosophers Karl Marx and Adam Smith; innovators like Henry Bessemer, Henry Ford, Robert Fulton, and Eli Whitney; financial wizards Andrew Carnegie and J. P. Morgan; and crusading journalists such as Upton Sinclair and Ida Tarbell. The volume includes more than fifty photographs, sources for further reading, a timeline, and an index.

Acknowledgments

The authors extend their thanks to U•X•L editor Matthew May, U•X•L senior editors Diane Sawinski, Larry Baker, and Julie Carnagie, and U•X•L publisher Tom Romig for their assistance throughout the production of this series. Thanks, too, to Judy Galens for lending her editorial talents in the form of proofreading. The editor wishes to thank Marco Di Vita of the Graphix Group for always working with flexibility, speed, and, above all, quality.

Comments and suggestions

We welcome your comments on *Industrial Revolution: Primary Sources* and suggestions for other topics in history to consider. Please write: Editors, *Industrial Revolution: Primary Sources,* U•X•L, 27500 Drake Road, Farmington Hills, Michigan, 48331-3535; call toll-free: 800-877-4253; fax to 248-699-8097; or send e-mail via www.gale.com.

Industrial Revolution Timeline

1702 Thomas Savery, inventor of a device that was the predecessor to the steam engine, writes *The Miner's Friend* in an effort to sway coal mine owners to use his invention.

1776 *An Inquiry into the Nature and Causes of the Wealth of Nations* by Adam Smith is published.

June 13, 1786 The *Leeds Intelligencer* and *Leeds Mercury* publish the "Yorkshire Cloth Workers' Petition," which warns that advances in machinery would result in workers losing their jobs. Five years later the Leeds Cloth Merchants publish an article in the same papers in support of mechanization.

1811 A group of textile workers in England known as the Luddites, concerned with the growing reliance on machinery in their factories, distributes a series of letters that call attention to the plight of workers and threaten factory owners.

January 1833 British Parliament member Michael Sadler issues *The Sadler Report, 1831–1832,* a review of child labor in British textile mills.

1835 Andrew Ure writes about the positive aspects of the factory system in his book *The Philosophy of Manufacturers.*

May 1, 1844 Samuel F. B. Morse sends the first telegraph message. Four years later, a telegraph message is sent from Washington, D.C., to the offices of the *New York Herald,* which prompts a *Herald* reporter to proclaim a new era of communication, a new "Age of Miracles."

1848 *The Communist Manifesto,* written by Karl Marx and his friend Frederich Engels, is published.

1849 Charlotte Brontë's novel *Shirley, a Tale,* about attacks on a factory by frustrated workers and the factory owner's struggle to protect his property, is published.

July 1869 J. D. B. Stillman publishes "The Last Tie," an account of the completion of the transcontinental railroad, in *Overland Monthly.*

October 31, 1881 Samuel Gompers publishes "Tenement-House Cigar Manufacture" in the magazine *New Yorker Volkszeitung.*

1885 Émile Zola's *Germinal,* a novel about working conditions of coal miners in northern France, is published.

June 1889 "The Gospel of Wealth," written by Andrew Carnegie, is published in *North American Review.*

September 14, 1901 Theodore Roosevelt becomes president of the United States upon the death of William McKinley.

1904 Associate Justice John Marshall Harlan writes the majority opinion for the U.S. Supreme Court in *Northern Securities Co.* v. *United States.* The decision upholds the right of the federal government to break up businesses that unfairly limit competition.

1906 Upton Sinclair's *The Jungle,* a novel about working conditions in Chicago, Illinois, meat-packing plants, is published.

March 27, 1911 William G. Shepherd writes an account of the Triangle Shirtwaist Factory disaster for the *Milwaukee Journal.*

1912   The pioneering social worker Jane Addams publishes her autobiography, *Twenty Years at Hull-House.*

March 1912   Child laborer Camella Teoli testifies in front of the U.S. House of Representatives regarding her experiences as a worker in a textile mill.

1912   Theodore Roosevelt runs for the presidency of the United States as the candidate of the Progressive Party, but is defeated by Democrat Woodrow Wilson in the general election.

Industrial
Revolution
Primary Sources

Economic Theory

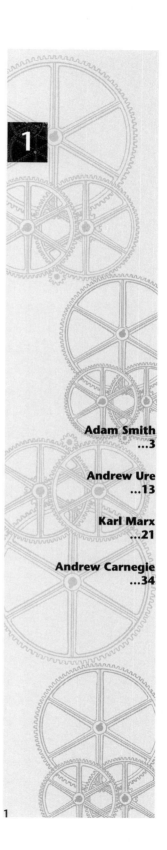

S tarting in England around 1750, the introduction of new machines powered by steam or by running water in streams and rivers changed the ways people had lived and worked for centuries. These changes, called the Industrial Revolution, were embraced by some people and rejected by others. The new machines, which were too big and too expensive for individual workers to install and operate in their homes, gave rise to factories, financed by a group of business owners who hired workers to run the machines. Some factory owners became very wealthy; industrialization was a new route to riches, along with international trade and owning land. At the same time, jobs once done by highly skilled workers, such as weaving, were transferred to factories, and the formerly independent workers became employees of the new factory owners.

The Industrial Revolution gave rise to a group of thinkers and writers who thought about the implications of these changes in work. Some writers, such as Adam Smith (1723–1790), writing in 1776, foresaw advantages for both factory owners and working people in the new arrangements.

Smith also saw a third player in the economy—the government, which had long adopted policies on foreign trade, especially, that might help or hinder the new move towards industrialization. Scottish professor Andrew Ure (1778–1857) argued that industrialization and factory life was a benefit to workers, and much better than attempting to make a living at farming. While Smith and Ure saw the potential good that might come from the rise of factories, other writers, such as Karl Marx (1818–1883), saw the disadvantages. Writing about seventy-five years later, Marx thought that factory workers should stage a violent revolution to seize control of the factories and run them on a democratic basis.

The accumulation of wealth was also an issue that grabbed attention during the Industrial Revolution. Andrew Carnegie (1835–1919), who rose from poor beginnings to become the leading steel manufacturer and one of the wealthiest individuals in the United States, thought that wealth was a good thing. Whereas most people could never hope to achieve great riches, the existence of a few wealthy individuals resulted in money being spent for cultural advancement (in painting and music, for example). The wealthy also served as inspiration for people who, in the future, might hope to succeed as Carnegie did. Of course, Carnegie's views might have been flavored by the fact that he was one of the few to achieve a degree of wealth that most workers could barely imagine.

Adam Smith

Excerpt from An Inquiry into the
Nature and Causes of the Wealth of Nations

Published in 1776

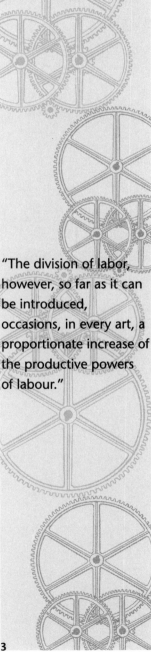

"The division of labor, however, so far as it can be introduced, occasions, in every art, a proportionate increase of the productive powers of labour."

Adam Smith (1723–1790) was one of the first people to write about what is now called economics, the way a people in a society make a living and spend money. Smith was a professor at the University of Glasgow in 1776 when he published his most famous work, *An Inquiry into the Nature and Causes of the Wealth of Nations,* usually called simply *The Wealth of Nations.* His topic was how the British government could increase the wealth of the country by adopting certain policies and avoiding others. Smith believed in laissez-faire (pronounced less-say-FAIR, a French term meaning "free to do") economics, relying on the free market to proceed without government interference. His book has been studied ever since, both by government officials and by economists (people who study how people and nations make a living).

One of Smith's concerns was how to improve the productivity of labor. (Productivity is the measure of how much value a person creates in a period of time, such as a week or a year. Smith thought the best way to maximize productivity was to let individuals focus on specific tasks and become very good at doing just one or two things, a theory he called the

Adam Smith's ground-breaking work is still studied by economists today. *Reproduced by permission of the Library of Congress.*

division of labor. The notion that workers should specialize in a single task was later used in setting up assembly lines to make complex objects, like a car, by letting each worker do just one thing, such as attach the wheels.

This selection from *The Wealth of Nations* comes from the very beginning of the book. The example Smith uses to illustrate his point is people who manufacture pins (like those used in sewing). Smith says that if an individual were to try to do the whole job of making pins—from pulling a piece of wire into a very thin strand to putting the head on the pin—the result might be producing one pin a day. But if ten people divided the task into its separate parts, together they could produce about forty-eight thousand pins a day—or about forty-eight hundred pins per individual.

Smith's example describes the way new factories were being set up at the beginning of the Industrial Revolution, the term used to describe the introduction of new water- or steam-powered machines in factories to replace work traditionally done by hand. The Industrial Revolution was getting started at the same time Smith was writing. In the new factories, work was reorganized in the way Smith recommended, with an individual worker assigned part of the overall task. (In the older methods, workers at home were responsible for the whole process of spinning yarn or weaving cloth, for example.) Smith wrote that the division of labor was an important reason that Britain was becoming wealthier than nations where traditional methods were used.

Smith thought farming was an exception to the idea of division of labor. One farmer usually did a variety of jobs as one season moved to the next. And for that reason, he wrote, British farming did not have an advantage over any other country's farming, whereas British manufacturing (where division of labor was the rule) enjoyed a huge advantage.

Things to remember while reading the excerpt from *The Wealth of Nations:*

- Smith's book was published in 1776, at the beginning of the Industrial Revolution. He had not yet seen the eventual results of the division of labor—how monotonous and boring jobs could become, or how factory owners would insist that workers stay on the job for twelve or sixteen hours a day, long after they were exhausted.

- Smith was thinking about how to increase the wealth of Great Britain as a whole society. His study on the division of labor was not so concerned with how much workers should be paid, although he took up this subject later in his book.

- In England in the 1700s, working people had very few political rights, and there was not much concern for their welfare. On the other hand, people who owned property—both land, used for farming, and equipment or factories—had a lot of rights. Smith was primarily concerned with how property owners should behave to increase the wealth of the country.

- Smith used the language and spelling of his time, which is preserved in this excerpt.

The Life of Adam Smith

Born in 1723 in Kirkcaldy, Scotland, Adam Smith was the only child of Adam Smith and Margaret Douglas.

A sickly but brilliant child, he was always attracted to books more than physical activity. He entered the University of Glasgow at age fourteen. Three years later, when he was seventeen, he went to Oxford University, where he stayed for seven years. He returned to Edinburgh, Scotland, in 1748.

His best-known work is *An Inquiry into the Nature and Causes of the Wealth of Nations* (1776), in which he advocates a system of competition rather than the highly regulated foreign trade prevalent at the time.

Smith thought taxes should be kept low, and that people should be free to exercise their own best judgment about how to conduct business, including foreign trade, which was highly regulated at the time he published *The Wealth of Nations.*

Adam Smith is sometimes called the father of modern economics, and many of his ideas are still promoted today.

Excerpt from The Wealth of Nations

*The greatest improvement in the productive powers of **labour**, and the greater part of the skill, **dexterity**, and judgment with which it is any where directed, or applied, seem to have been the effects of the division of labour.*

*The effects of the division of labour, in the general business of society, will be more easily understood, by considering in what manner it operates in some particular **manufactures**. It is commonly supposed to be carried furthest in some very **trifling** ones; not perhaps that it really is carried further in them than in others of more importance: but in those trifling manufactures which are destined to supply the small wants of but a small number of people, the whole number of workmen must necessarily be small; and those employed in every different branch of the work can often be collected into the same workhouse, and placed at once under the view of the spectator.*

In those great manufactures, on the contrary, which are destined to supply the great wants of the great body of the people, every different branch of the work employs so great a number of workmen, that it is impossible to collect them all into the same workhouse. We can seldom see more, at one time, than those employed in one single branch. Though in such manufactures, therefore, the work may really be divided into a much greater number of parts, than in those of a more trifling nature, the division is not near so obvious, and has accordingly been much less observed.

*To take an example, therefore, from a very trifling manufacture; but one in which the division of labour has been very often taken notice of, the trade of the pin-maker; a workman not educated to this business (which the division of labour has **rendered** a distinct trade), nor acquainted with the use of the machinery employed in it (to the invention of which the same division of labour has probably given occasion), could scarce, perhaps, with his utmost industry, make one pin in a day, and certainly could not make twenty. But in the way in which this business is now carried on, not only the whole work is a peculiar trade, but it is divided into a number of branches, of which the greater part are likewise peculiar trades. One man*

Labour: British spelling of labor; work.

Dexterity: Quickness; strength.

Manufactures: Factories.

Trifling: Minor.

Rendered: Produced.

draws out the wire, another **straights** it, a third cuts it, a fourth points it, a fifth grinds it at the top for receiving the head; to make the head requires two or three distinct operations; to put it on, is a peculiar business, to whiten the pins is another; it is even a trade by itself to put them into the paper; and the important business of making a pin is, in this manner, divided into about eighteen distinct operations, which, in some **manufactories**, are all performed by distinct hands, though in others the same man will sometimes perform two or three of them. I have seen a small manufactory of this kind where ten men only were employed, and where some of them consequently performed two or three distinct operations. But though they were very poor, and therefore but indifferently accommodated with the necessary machinery, they could, when they exerted themselves, make among them about twelve pounds of pins in a day. There are in a pound upwards of four thousand pins of a **middling** size. Those ten persons, therefore, could make among them upwards of forty-eight thousand pins in a day. Each person, therefore, making a tenth part of forty-eight thousand pins, might be considered as making four thousand eight hundred pins in a day. But if they had all **wrought** separately and independently, and without any of them having been educated to this peculiar business, they certainly could not each of them have made twenty, perhaps not one pin in a day; that is certainly, not the two hundred and fortieth, perhaps not the four thousand eight hundredth part of what they are at present capable of performing, in consequence of a proper division and combination of their different operations.

In every other art and manufacture, the effects of the division of labour are similar to what they are in this very trifling one; though, in many of them, the labour can neither be so much subdivided, nor reduced to so great a simplicity of operation. The division of labour, however, so far as it can be introduced, occasions, in every art, a proportionate increase of the productive powers of labour. The separation of different trades and employments from one another, seems to have taken place, in consequence of this advantage. This separation too is generally carried furthest in those countries which enjoy the highest degree of industry and improvement; what is the work of one man in a **rude** state of society, being generally that of several in an improved one. In every improved society, the farmer is generally nothing but a farmer; the manufacturer, nothing but a manufacturer. The labour too which is necessary to produce any one complete manufacture, is almost always divided among a great number of hands. How many different trades are

Straights: Straightens.

Manufactories: An early form of the word "factories." The word is related to the word "manufacturing," meaning literally "to make by hand," even though machines have come to be involved.

Middling: Middle, or medium.

Wrought: Made.

Rude: Primitive.

employed in each branch of the linen and woollen manufacturers, from the growers of the flax and the wool, to the bleachers and smoothers of the linen, or to the dyers and dressers of the cloth! The nature of agriculture, indeed, does not admit of so many subdivisions of labour, nor of so complete a separation of one business from another, as manufactures. It is impossible to separate so entirely, the business of the **grazier** from that of the corn-farmer, as the trade of carpenter is commonly separated from that of the smith. The **spinner** is almost always a distinct person from the **weaver**; but the **ploughman**, the **harrower**, the sower of the seed, and the reaper of the corn, are often the same. The occasions for those different sorts of labour returning with the different seasons of the year, it is impossible that one man should be constantly employed in any one of them. This impossibility of making so complete and entire a separation of all the different branches of labour employed in agriculture, is perhaps the reason why the improvement of the productive powers of labour in this art, does not always keep pace with their improvement in manufactures. The most **opulent** nations, indeed, generally excel all their neighbours in agriculture as well as in manufacturers; but they are commonly more distinguished by their superiority in the latter than in the former. Their lands are in general better **cultivated**, and having more labour and expence bestowed upon them, produce more in proportion to the extent and natural **fertility** of the ground. But this superiority of produce is seldom much more than in proportion to the superiority of labour and expence. In agriculture, the labour of the rich country is not always much more productive than that of the poor; or, at least, it is never so much more productive, as it commonly is in manufactures. The corn of the rich country, therefore, will not always, in the same degree of goodness, come cheaper to market than that of the poor. The corn of Poland, in the same degree of goodness, is as cheap as that of France, **notwithstanding** the superior opulence and improvement of the latter country. The corn of France is, in the corn provinces, fully as good, and in most years nearly about the same price with the corn of England, though, in opulence and improvement, France is perhaps inferior to England. The corn-lands of England, however, are better cultivated than those of France, and the corn-lands of France are said to be much better cultivated than those of Poland. But though the poor country, notwithstanding the inferiority of its cultivation, can, in some measure, rival the rich in the cheapness and goodness of its corn, it can pretend to no such competition in its manufactures; at least if those manufactures suit

Grazier: A farmer who puts out cattle to feed, or graze, on grass.

Spinner: One who spins, or makes yarn from raw materials.

Weaver: One who makes cloth from yarn.

Ploughman: One who operates a plow.

Harrower: Planter.

Opulent: Wealthy.

Cultivated: Prepared.

Fertility: The richness of the soil.

Notwithstanding: Ignoring.

the soil, climate, and situation of the rich country. The silks of France are better and cheaper than those of England, because the silk manufacture, at least under the present high duties upon the importation of raw silk, does not so well suit the climate of England as that of France. But the hard-ware and the coarse woollens of England are beyond all comparison superior to those of France, and much cheaper too in the same degree of goodness. In Poland there are said to be scarce any manufactures of any kind, a few of those coarser household manufactures excepted, without which no country can well **subsist**.

This great increase of the quantity of work, which, in consequence of the division of labour, the same number of people are capable of performing, is owing to three different circumstances; first, to the increase of dexterity in every particular workman; secondly, to the saving of the time which is commonly lost in passing from one **species** of work to another; and lastly, to the invention of a great number of machines which **facilitate** and **abridge** labour, and enable one man to do the work of many.

First, the improvement of the dexterity of the workman necessarily increases the quantity of the work he can perform; and the division of labour, by reducing every man's business to some one simple operation, and by making this operation the sole employment of his life, necessarily increases very much the dexterity of the workman. A common smith, who, though accustomed to handle the hammer, has never been used to make nails, if upon some particular occasion he is obliged to attempt it, will scarce, I am assured, be able to make above two or three hundred nails in a day, and those too very bad ones. A smith who has been accustomed to make nails, but whose sole or principal business has not been that of a nailer, can seldom with his utmost **diligence** make more than eight hundred or a thousand nails in a day. I have seen several boys under twenty years of age who had never exercised any other trade but that of making nails, and who, when they exerted themselves, could make, each of them, upwards of two thousand three hundred nails in a day. The making of a nail, however, is by no means one of the simplest operations. The same person blows the **bellows**, stirs or mends the fire as there is occasion, heats the iron, and **forges** every part of the nail: In forging the head too he is obliged to change his tools. The different operations into which the making of a pin, or of a metal button, is subdivided, are all of them much more simple, and the dexterity of the person, of whose life it has been the sole business to perform them, is usually much greater. The rapidity with

Subsist: Survive.

Species: Type.

Facilitate: Make easier.

Abridge: Shorten.

Diligence: Effort.

Bellows: A device that blows air into a chamber to build a fire.

Forges: Forms.

which some of the operations of those manufactures are performed, exceeds what the human hand could, by those who had never seen them, be supposed capable of acquiring.

Secondly, the advantage which is gained by saving the time commonly lost in passing from one sort of work to another, is much greater than we should at first view be apt to imagine it. It is impossible to pass very quickly from one kind of work to another, that is carried on in a different place, and with quite different tools. A country weaver, who cultivates a small farm, must lose a good deal of time in passing from his **loom** to the field, and from the field to his loom. When the two trades can be carried on in the same workhouse, the loss of time is no doubt much less. It is even in this case, however, very considerable. A man commonly **saunters** a little in turning his hand from one sort of employment to another. When he first begins the new work he is seldom very keen and hearty; his mind, as they say, does not go to it, and for some time he rather trifles than applies to good purpose. The habit of sauntering and of **indolent** careless application, which is naturally, or rather necessarily acquired by every country workman who is **obliged** to change his work and his tools every half hour, and to apply his hand in twenty different ways almost every day of his life; renders him almost always **slothful** and lazy, and incapable of any vigorous application even on the most pressing occasions. Independent, therefore, of his **deficiency** in point of dexterity, this cause alone must always reduce considerably the quantity of work which he is capable of performing.

Thirdly, and lastly, every body must be sensible how much labour is facilitated and abridged by the application of proper machinery. It is unnecessary to give any example. I shall only observe, therefore, that the invention of all those machines by which labour is so much facilitated and abridged, seems to have been originally owing to the division of labour. Men are much more likely to discover easier and readier methods of attaining any object, when the whole attention of their minds is directed towards that single object, than when it is **dissipated** among a great variety of things. But in consequence of the division of labour, the whole of every man's attention comes naturally to be directed towards some one very simple object. It is naturally to be expected, therefore, that some one or other of those who are employed in each particular branch of labour should soon find out easier and readier methods of performing their own particular work, wherever the nature of it admits of such im-

Loom: a machine used to weave yarn into cloth.

Saunters: Walks slowly.

Indolent: Lazy.

Obliged: Required.

Slothful: Sloppy.

Deficiency: Lacking.

Dissipated: Distributed.

*provement. A great part of the machines made use of in those man-
ufactures in which labour is most subdivided, were originally the inventions of common workmen, who, being each of them employed
in some very simple operation, naturally turned their thoughts towards finding out easier and readier methods of performing it. Whoever has been much accustomed to visit such manufacturers, must
frequently have been **shewn** very pretty machines, which were the
inventions of such workmen, in order to facilitate and quicken their
own particular part of the work. In the first **fire-engines**, a boy was
constantly employed to open and shut alternately the communication between the boiler and the cylinder, according as the piston either ascended or descended. One of those boys, who loved to play
with his companions, observed that, by tying a string from the handle of the valve which opened this communication to another part
of the machine, the valve would open and shut without his assistance, and leave him at liberty to **divert** himself with his play-fel-
lows. One of the greatest improvements that has been made upon
this machine, since it was first invented, was in this manner the discovery of a boy who wanted to save his own labour.*

Shewn: Shown.

Fire-engines: Steam engines.

Divert: Amuse.

What happened next ...

Adam Smith's ideas were already being widely adopted when he wrote his book. These practices became increas-
ingly widespread, and Smith was quoted (and still is quoted)
as an authority on the best way to organize manufacturing.

Smith died in 1790. Efforts by factory owners to
speed up production, and to keep down the cost of hiring
workers, led to horrific abuses in the early 1800s. Workers—
including children—were required to be on the job for twelve
or more hours a day, with few breaks. Exhaustion, and the
monotony of doing the same task repeatedly, led to accidents
that caused serious injury or even death.

Adam Smith did not live to observe the nature of factories in the 1800s; the abuses there resulted in laws and regulations passed by the British Parliament to protect children,

women, and other workers. Would he still have believed in laissez-faire had he seen these conditions?

Did you know ...

Adam Smith was an acquaintance of James Watt, the man who perfected the steam engine, which was central to the Industrial Revolution. Smith and Watt belonged to a group of individuals who called themselves the Lunar Society of Birmingham—or, sometimes, the Lunaticks—because they met for dinner on nights when the moon was full so that they could see their way home by the moonlight. Their club, which included a dozen other members, met almost every month for more than thirty years.

For more information

Books

Macfarlane, Alan. *The Riddle of the Modern World: Of Liberty, Wealth and Equality*. New York: St. Martin's Press, 2000.

Meek, Ronald L. *Smith, Marx, and After: Ten Essays in the Development of Economic Thought*. New York: Wiley, 1977.

Ross, Ian Simpson. *The Life of Adam Smith*. New York: Oxford University Press, 1995.

Smith, Adam. *An Inquiry into the Nature and Causes of the Wealth of Nations*. 1776. Reprint, New York: T. Nelson and Sons, 1870.

Andrew Ure

Excerpt from **The Philosophy of Manufactures; or, an Exposition of the Scientific, Moral, and Commercial Economy of the Factory System of Great Britain**

Published in 1835

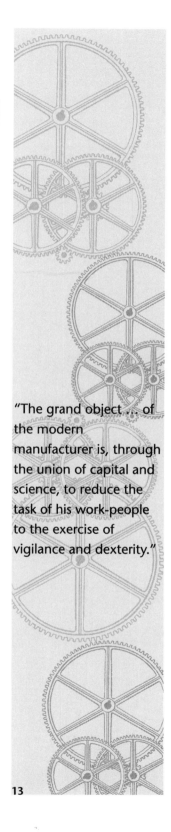

"The grand object ... of the modern manufacturer is, through the union of capital and science, to reduce the task of his work-people to the exercise of vigilance and dexterity."

By 1835 the Industrial Revolution—the process of introducing machines into manufacturing and of building new factories—was well established in Britain. Three years earlier, in 1832, a member of Parliament, Michael Sadler (see entry), had published a report documenting the abuse of children working in factories. Many factory workers had joined the Chartist movement, an effort to persuade Parliament to give more people the right to vote (at the time, only men with a minimum amount of property were allowed to vote) and to pass laws to guarantee a minimum wage and maximum number of hours people cold be required to work. (The Chartist movement lasted from 1838 to 1848, but it never persuaded Parliament to act.)

Despite the long hours and dangerous working conditions, the Industrial Revolution also had its positive aspects. Andrew Ure (1778–1857), a professor at the University of Glasgow in Scotland, laid them out in a book titled *The Philosophy of Manufactures; or, an Exposition of the Scientific, Moral, and Commercial Economy of the Factory System of Great Britain,* published in 1835. In this excerpt from his book, Ure points out what he saw as benefits to the country as a whole, such as an overall increase in wealth and greater productivity (more value produced by one person in a given period of time), while ignoring complaints by workers about low pay and harsh living conditions. Ure argues that factory workers were actually better off under industrialization (the system of machines and factories) than they would be living on tiny plots in the countryside, trying to make a living as farmers (as many factory workers had once done).

Things to remember while reading the excerpt from *The Philosophy of Manufactures:*

- Ure's view reflects the opinions and interests of Britain's business owners. They were a new class in British society, their wealth gained from the introduction of machines and factories that marked the Industrial Revolution. Many of these business owners had gained political influence just three years before Ure wrote his essay, as a result of the Reform Act of 1832. That act changed the British system of electing members of Parliament and gave more political influence to urban business owners at the expense of the older class of landowners.

- Perhaps in an effort to defend factory owners, Ure argues (not always convincingly) that workers should look on the bright side. For example, in response to complaints that workers were not allowed to take breaks, Ure says that breaks taken in the old system, by home-based skilled workers, only resulted in wasted time and therefore lower pay. Furthermore, he says, the steam engines that powered factory equipment made work easier than tasks using the older hand-driven equipment.

- Ure foresees the day when workers will become "mere overlookers of machines," doing jobs that do not require much skill. He sees an advantage in eliminating the need for highly skilled workers, such as weavers, because they tend to be difficult to work with and demand more money. This, in turn, drives up the price of manufactured goods.

- In Ure's view, people working in factories would in some respects become part of a mechanical process for turning out goods (he was primarily talking about textiles—yarn and fabric—in his book, but his principles apply to other industries as well). His view was shared by many business owners of his time.

- Ure argues from the viewpoint of society in general, and Britain in particular. In the international struggle between nations to achieve power and strength, the Industrial Revolution helped Britain become the wealthiest and most powerful country in the nineteenth century, even if many British workers suffered in the process.

Excerpt from
The Philosophy of Manufactures

This island [England] is **pre-eminent** among civilized nations for the **prodigious** development of its factory wealth, and has been therefore long viewed with a jealous admiration by foreign powers. This very pre-eminence, however, has been contemplated in a very different light by many influential members of our own community, and has been even denounced by them as the certain origin of innumerable evils to the people, and of revolutionary **convulsions** to the state. If the affairs of the kingdom be wisely administered, I believe such **allegations** and fears will prove to be groundless, and to proceed more from the envy of one ancient and powerful order of the **commonwealth**, towards another suddenly grown into political importance [business owners], than from the nature of things....

The blessings which **physio-mechanical science** has bestowed on society, and the means it has still in store for **ameliorating** the lot of mankind, have been too little dwelt upon; while, on the other hand, it has been accused of lending itself to the rich **capitalists** as an instrument for **harassing** the poor, and of exacting from the **operative** an **accelerated** rate of work. It has been said, for example, that the steam-engine now drives the power-looms with such **velocity** as to urge on their attendant weavers at the same rapid pace; but that the hand-weaver, not being subjected to this restless agent, can throw his **shuttle** and move his **treddles** at his convenience. There is, however, this difference in the two cases, that in the factory, every member of

Pre-eminent: Best; ruling.

Prodigious: Extraordinary.

Convulsions: Violent disturbances; fits.

Allegations: Charges; accusations.

Commonwealth: The aristocracy.

Physio-mechancial science: Machinery.

Ameliorating: Improving.

Capitalists: Business owners.

Harassing: Bothering.

Operative: Worker.

Accelerated: Faster.

Velocity: Speed.

Shuttle: A part of a hand loom.

Treddles: Parts of a hand loom.

Despite Andrew Ure's assertion that technological advances made work easier for laborers and was a generous gift to employees, many children endured difficult work for low wages. *Reproduced by permission of the Library of Congress.*

Gratis: Latin word meaning "free."

Irksome: Annoying.

Hovel: Small shack or house.

Philanthropic: Charitable.

the loom is so adjusted, that the driving force leaves the attendant nearly nothing at all to do, certainly no muscular fatigue to sustain, while it procures for him good, unfailing wages, besides a healthy workshop **gratis**: whereas the non-factory weaver, having everything to execute by muscular exertion, finds the labour **irksome**, makes in consequence innumerable short pauses, separately of little account, but great when added together; earns therefore proportionally low wages, while he loses his health by poor diet and the dampness of his **hovel**....

The constant aim and effect of scientific improvement in manufactures are **philanthropic**, as they tend to relieve the workmen either from niceties of adjustment which exhaust his mind and fatigue his eyes, or from painful repetition of efforts which distort or wear out his frame. At every step of each manufacturing process described in this volume the humanity of science will be manifest....

In its precise acceptation, the Factory system is of recent origin, and may claim England for its birthplace. The mills for throwing silk, or making **organzine** which were mounted centuries ago in several of the Italian states, and furtively transferred to this country by **Sir Thomas Lombe** in 1718, contained indeed certain elements of a factory, and probably suggested some hints of those grander and more complex combinations of self-acting machines, which were first embodied half a century later in our cotton manufacture by **Richard Arkwright,** assisted by gentlemen of Derby, well acquainted with its celebrated silk establishment. But the spinning of an entangled flock of fibres into a smooth thread, which constitutes the main operation with cotton, is in silk **superfluous;** being already performed by the unerring instinct of a worm, which leaves to human art the simple task of doubling and twisting its regular filaments. The apparatus requisite for this purpose is more elementary, and calls for few of those gradations of machinery which are needed in the carding, drawing, roving, and spinning processes of a cotton-mill.

When the first **water-frames** for spinning cotton were erected at Cromford, in the romantic valley of the Derwent [England], about sixty years ago, mankind were little aware of the mighty revolution which the new system of labour was destined by Providence to achieve, not only in the structure of British society, but in the fortunes of the world at large. Arkwright alone had the **sagacity** to discern, and the boldness to predict in glowing language, how vastly productive human industry would become, when no longer proportioned in its results to muscular effort, which is by its nature fitful and **capricious,** but when made to consist in the task of guiding the work of mechanical fingers and arms, regularly impelled with great velocity by some **indefatigable** physical power. What his judgment so clearly led him to perceive, his energy of will enabled him to realize with such rapidity and success, as would have done honour to the most influential individuals, but were truly wonderful in that obscure and indigent **artisan....**

The principle of the factory system then is, to substitute mechanical science for hand skill, and the **partition** of a process into its essential constituents, for the division or graduation of labour among artisans. On the handicraft plan, labour more or less skilled was usually the most expensive element of production ... but on the automatic plan, skilled labour gets progressively superseded, and will, eventually, be replaced by mere overlookers of machines.

By the infirmity of human nature it happens, that the more skilful the workman, the more self-willed and **intractable** he is apt to

Organzine: Silk yarn.

Sir Thomas Lombe: (1685–1792) Inventor of the spinning frame, a machine for weaving yarn.

Richard Arkwright: (1732–1792) An inventor who improved upon the spinning frame.

Superfluous: Exceeding what is necessary.

Water-frames: Machines used for spinning yarn.

Sagacity: Wise foresight.

Capricious: Subject to chance.

Indefatigable: Tireless.

Artisan: Craftsman.

Partition: Wall; separation.

Intractable: Cannot be moved; stubborn.

become, and, of course, the less fit a component of a mechanical system, in which, by occasional irregularities, he may do great damage to the whole. The grand object therefore of the modern manufacturer is, through the union of capital and science, to reduce the task of his work-people to the exercise of vigilance and **dexterity,**—faculties, when concentrated to one process, speedily brought to perfection in the young. In the infancy of mechanical engineering, a machine-factory displayed the division of labour in manifold gradations—the file, the drill, the lathe, having each its different workmen in the order of skill: but the dextrous hands of the filer and driller are now superseded by the planing, the key groove cutting, and the drilling-machines; and those of the iron and brass turners, by the self-acting slide-lathe....

It is, in fact, the constant aim and tendency of every improvement in machinery to supersede human labour altogether, or to diminish its cost, by substituting the industry of women and children for that of men; or that of ordinary labourers for trained artisans. In most of the water-twist, or **throstle** cotton-mills, the spinning is entirely managed by females of sixteen years and upwards. The effect of substituting the self-acting mule for the common mule, is to discharge the greater part of the men spinners, and to retain adolescents and children. The proprietor of a factory near Stockport states, in evidence to the commissioners, that, by such substitution, he would save 50 pounds [unit of British money] a week in wages in consequence of dispensing with nearly forty male spinners, at about 25 shillings [unit of British money] of wages each....

Steam-engines furnish the means not only of their support but of their multiplication. They create a vast demand for fuel; and, while they lend their powerful arms to drain the pits and to raise the coals, they call into employment multitudes of miners, engineers, shipbuilders, and sailors, and cause the construction of canals and railways. Thus therefore, in enabling these rich fields of industry to be cultivated to the utmost, they leave thousands of fine **arable** fields free for the production of food to man, which must have been otherwise allotted to the food of horses. Steam-engines moreover, by the cheapness and steadiness of their action, fabricate cheap goods, and **procure** in their exchange a liberal supply of the necessaries and comforts of life produced in foreign lands.

Improvements in the machinery have a three-fold bearing:

Ist. They make it possible to fabricate some articles which, but for them, could not be fabricated at all.

Dexterity: Quickness; strength.

Throstle: Old spinning machine.

Arable: Able to produce crops.

Procure: Acquire.

2nd. They enable an operative to turn out a greater quantity of work than he could before,—time, labour, and quality of work remaining constant.

3rd. They effect a substitution of labour comparatively unskilled, for that which is more skilled.

What happened next ...

Some of Andrew Ure's predictions came to pass. The industrial era did result in a much greater total output than had been possible previously. But workers did not agree to becoming "mere overlookers of machines." Both skilled and unskilled workers resisted this role and organized themselves into labor unions to demand greater pay and improved working conditions.

Ure also correctly forecast the gradual reduction in the cost of goods, at least in comparison to wages. Workers eventually received higher wages, but the cost of manufactured goods did not rise in proportion. In the end, the standard of living for workers and business owners alike rose enormously as a result of the continued success of the Industrial Revolution.

For more information

Books

Langley, Andrew. *The Industrial Revolution.* New York: Viking, 1994.

McPherson, Natalie. *Machines and Economic Growth: The Implications for Growth Theory of the History of the Industrial Revolution.* Westport, CT: Greenwood Press, 1994.

Stalcup, Brenda, ed. *The Industrial Revolution.* San Diego: Greenhaven Press, 2002.

Ure, Andrew. *The Philosophy of Manufactures; or, an Exposition of the Scientific, Moral, and Commercial Economy of the Factory System of Great Britain.* 1835. Reprint, New York: B. Franklin, 1969.

Web Sites

"Andrew Ure: The Philosophy of the Manufacturers, 1835." *Modern History Sourcebook*. http://www.fordham.edu/halsall/mod/1835ure.html (accessed on April 11, 2003).

Karl Marx

Excerpt from **The Communist Manifesto**

Published in 1848; translation from German into English by Helen Macfarlane published in *The Red Republican*, June–November 1850

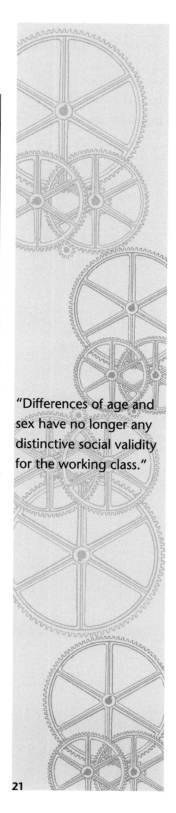

"Differences of age and sex have no longer any distinctive social validity for the working class."

Whether you agree with it or detest its message, there is little doubt that *The Communist Manifesto* is one of the most influential documents produced during the Industrial Revolution. It is the core document of communism, a form of government in which all the people own property, including both land and capital, in common. The tension between communisim and capitalist democracy was at the heart of the forty-five-year-long Cold War (1945–90) between the United States and the Soviet Union (now the Russian Federation). Communism, and the fight against it, was one of the major features of the twentieth century throughout the industrialized world, as well as in the developing countries of Africa and Asia.

When it was implemented in Russia as a result of the Bolshevik Revolution in 1917, communism resulted in a dictatorship that seemed in most respects much worse than the conditions that inspired it. Individual political freedoms were crushed completely, and the economic hardships of workers in communist countries were far worse than their counterparts in countries like the United States, which allowed private property and limited regulation of businesses. In 1991,

The title page of the original German-language version of *The Communist Manifesto. Reproduced by permission of Hulton Archive.*

however, Russia ceased being governed by communists, as non-communists seized power peacefully in the wake of an economic crisis. The change in government seemed to signal the collapse of the views of German philosopher Karl Marx (1818–1883) as well.

In the United States, Marx and his philosophy were feared and detested for most of the twentieth century. For forty-six years following World War II (1939–45), the United States was in the forefront of an international struggle between communism and capitalism (the system of private ownership of business). In the 1950s, Americans could lose their jobs for belonging to the Communist Party in the United States because such membership was viewed as unpatriotic, and communism was seen as the enemy of everything Americans held dear, including private property and religious beliefs. In communist countries, even worse fates, such as execution or deportation to remote labor camps, befell people who advocated an end to communism in favor of capitalism.

The ideas behind communism were an important part of the Industrial Revolution, the period when machines and factories were being introduced, changing the nature of work for millions of people. *The Communist Manifesto* was written in 1848, a time of widespread unrest in Europe. As Marx described in the document, crowded cities, filled with people working in factories, were characteristic of the Industrial Revolution. So too was the fact that many of these workers had barely enough money to live on. Loss of a job meant loss of food and housing, almost overnight. Even in the twenty-first century, workers living in the developing countries of Asia and Africa, which do not have industries to generate wealth, often experience the same desperate conditions that were typical of Europe and the United States in the period between 1850 and 1900. It is perhaps not so surprising that the message of Marx still has appeal in these countries.

Things to remember while reading the excerpt from *The Communist Manifesto:*

- *The Communist Manifesto* was written at the beginning of 1848. It was a year in Europe when industrial workers staged riots and revolutions in several cities, including Paris, France; Vienna, Austria; and Berlin, Germany. Marx was writing his manifesto (a statement of principles or intentions) as a political document designed to attract members to his political party, called the Communist League, one of many political parties competing for support from workers.

- For the most part, the economies of Europe in the 1840s were quite different from today. Wealthy individuals typically owned one modest-size factory. Large companies with factories in many countries were unknown. Many companies were family owned, whereas in the twenty-first century, industrial enterprises have many owners who have invested in a corporation, which is a kind of artificial person that the law recognizes as the owner of property. Thus, when Marx writes about the bourgeoisie (pronounced bourzh-wah-ZEE), he is writing about a specific and fairly large number of individuals and families who owned factories and other related enterprises and who worked together politically to try to make sure governments passed laws that were in their interest. Marx saw politics as a struggle between these property-owning individuals and the workers they hired, whom he called the proletariat.

- Marx goes to some length to describe how the class of factory owners—the bourgeoisie—had already carried out a revolution of their own. That revolution was what we call the Industrial Revolution, the rise of large factories and the disappearance of small workshops owned by skilled workers, such as weavers and blacksmiths. The Industrial Revolution also involved the migration of millions of people from the countryside and small towns to big cities where the new factories were located. Marx said people should not fear revolution since revolutions were natural in the course of history, and a communist revolution would be both natural and the inevitable result of the Industrial Revolution.

Excerpt from The Communist Manifesto

A **spectre** is haunting Europe—the spectre of **communism**. All the powers of old Europe have entered into a holy alliance to **exorcise** this spectre: Pope and **Tsar**, Metternich [Prince Klemens von Metternich (1773–1859), political leader of Austria] and Guizot, [François Guizot (1787–1874), leader of France]: French Radicals and German police-spies.

Where is the party in opposition that has not been **decried** as communistic by its opponents in power? Where is the opposition that has not hurled back the branding **reproach** of communism, against the more advanced opposition parties, as well as against its reactionary adversaries?

Two things result from this fact:

I. Communism is already acknowledged by all European powers to be itself a power.

II. It is high time that Communists should openly, in the face of the whole world, publish their views, their aims, their tendencies, and meet this nursery tale of the spectre of communism with a **manifesto** of the party itself.

To this end, Communists of various nationalities have assembled in London and sketched the following manifesto, to be published in the English, French, German, Italian, Flemish and Danish languages.

Bourgeois and Proletarians

The history of all hitherto existing society is the history of class struggles.

Freeman and slave, **patrician** and **plebian lord** and **serf, guild-master** and **journeyman**, in a word, oppressor and oppressed, stood in constant opposition to one another, carried on an uninterrupted, now hidden, now open fight, a fight that each time ended, either in a revolutionary **reconstitution** of society at large, or in the common ruin of the contending classes.

Spectre: Ghost.

Communism: A political and economic system in which property is owned by the state.

Exorcise: Get rid of.

Tsar: Ruler of Russia.

Decried: Criticized.

Reproach: Criticism.

Manifesto: A written declaration of principles and objectives.

Patrician: Ancient Roman aristocrat.

Plebian: Ancient Roman commoner.

Lord: Landowner.

Serf: Landless peasant.

Guild-master: Boss.

Journeyman: Employee.

Reconstitution: Change.

The philosophy of Karl Marx spread globally, as evidenced by these members of China's Red Guard Movement, rallying in support of Marxist theory and communism.
Reproduced by permission of AP/Wide World Photos.

In the earlier ***epochs*** of history, we find almost everywhere a complicated arrangement of society into various orders, a manifold ***gradation*** of social rank. In ancient Rome we have patricians, knights, plebians, slaves; in the Middle Ages, ***feudal*** lords, ***vassals***, guild-masters, journeymen, ***apprentices***, serfs; in almost all of these classes, again, subordinate gradations.

The modern ***bourgeois*** society that has sprouted from the ruins of feudal society has not done away with class ***antagonisms***. It has

Epochs: Eras.

Gradation: Layering.

Feudal: Ruling.

Vassals: Underlings; subordinates.

Apprentices: Those who work under a skilled professional to learn a trade.

Bourgeois: Middle class.

Antagonisms: Conflicts.

but established new classes, new conditions of oppression, new forms of struggle in place of the old ones.

*Our epoch, the epoch of the bourgeoisie, possesses, however, this distinct feature: it has simplified class antagonisms. Society as a whole is more and more splitting up into two great hostile camps, into two great classes directly facing each other—bourgeoisie and **proletariat**.*

*From the serfs of the Middle Ages sprang the chartered burghers of the earliest towns. From these **burgesses** the first elements of the bourgeoisie were developed.*

*The discovery of America, the rounding of the Cape, opened up fresh ground for the rising bourgeoisie. The East-Indian and Chinese markets, the **colonisation** of America, trade with the colonies, the increase in the means of exchange and in **commodities** generally, gave to commerce, to navigation, to industry, an impulse never before known, and thereby, to the revolutionary element in the tottering feudal society, a rapid development.*

*The feudal system of industry, in which industrial production was monopolized by closed **guilds**, now no longer suffices for the growing wants of the new markets. The manufacturing system took its place. The guild-masters were pushed aside by the manufacturing middle class; division of labor between the different corporate guilds vanished in the face of division of labor in each single workshop.*

Meantime, the markets kept ever growing, the demand ever rising. Even manufacturers no longer sufficed. Thereupon, steam and machinery revolutionized industrial production. The place of manufacture was taken by the giant, MODERN INDUSTRY; the place of the industrial middle class by industrial millionaires, the leaders of the whole industrial armies, the modern bourgeois.

*Modern industry has established the world market, for which the discovery of America paved the way. This market has given an immense development to commerce, to navigation, to communication by land. This development has, in turn, reacted on the extension of industry; and in proportion as industry, commerce, navigation, railways extended, in the same proportion the bourgeoisie developed, increased its **capital**, and pushed into the background every class handed down from the Middle Ages.*

We see, therefore, how the modern bourgeoisie is itself the product of a long course of development, of a series of revolutions in the modes of production and of exchange.

Proletariat: Working class.

Burgesses: Town representatives.

Colonisation: Establishment of a colony in an unsettled land.

Commodities: Products.

Guilds: Association of merchants or craftspeople.

Capital: Money; resources.

Each step in the development of the bourgeoisie was accompanied by a corresponding political advance in that class. An **oppressed** class under the sway of the feudal nobility, an armed and self-governing association of medieval **commune**: here independent urban republic (as in Italy and Germany); there taxable **"third estate"** of the monarchy (as in France); afterward, in the period of manufacturing proper, serving either the semi-feudal or the absolute **monarchy** as a **counterpoise** against the nobility, and, in fact, cornerstone of the great monarchies in general—the bourgeoisie has at last, since the establishment of Modern Industry and of the world market, conquered for itself, in the modern representative state, exclusive political sway. The executive of the modern state is but a committee for managing the common affairs of the whole bourgeoisie.

The bourgeoisie, historically, has played a most revolutionary part.

The bourgeoisie, wherever it has got the upper hand, has put an end to all feudal, patriarchal, **idyllic** relations. It has pitilessly **torn asunder** the **motley** feudal ties that bound man to his "natural superiors," and has left no other **nexus** between man and man than naked self-interest, than callous "cash payment." It has drowned out the most heavenly ecstasies of religious fervor, of **chivalrous** enthusiasm, of **philistine** sentimentalism, in the icy water of **egotistical** calculation. It has resolved personal worth into exchange value, and in place of the numberless indefeasible chartered freedoms, has set up that single, unconscionable freedom—Free Trade. In one word, for exploitation, veiled by religious and political illusions, it has substituted naked, shameless, direct, brutal exploitation.

The bourgeoisie has stripped of its halo every occupation hitherto honored and looked up to with reverent awe. It has converted the physician, the lawyer, the priest, the poet, the man of science, into its paid wage laborers.

The bourgeoisie has torn away from the family its sentimental veil, and has reduced the family relation into a mere money relation.

The bourgeoisie has disclosed how it came to pass that the brutal display of vigor in the Middle Ages, which reactionaries so much admire, found its fitting complement in the most slothful **indolence**. It has been the first to show what man's activity can bring about. It has accomplished wonders far surpassing Egyptian pyramids, Roman

Oppressed: Forcibly dominated.

Commune: Town.

Third Estate: People who are not clergy or aristocrats.

Monarchy: Political system in which a state is ruled by a monarch.

Counterpoise: Balance.

Idyllic: Untroubled.

Torn asunder: Ripped apart.

Motley: Diverse.

Nexus: Connection.

Chivalrous: Considerate and courteous.

Philistine: Unsophisticated.

Egotistical: Self-absorbed.

Indolence: Laziness.

*aqueducts, and Gothic cathedrals; it has conducted expeditions that put in the shade all former **exoduses** of nations and crusades.*

*The bourgeoisie cannot exist without constantly revolutionizing the instruments of production, and thereby the relations of production, and with them the whole relations of society. Conservation of the old modes of production in unaltered form, was, on the contrary, the first condition of existence for all earlier industrial classes. Constant revolutionizing of production, uninterrupted disturbance of all social conditions, everlasting uncertainty and agitation distinguish the bourgeois epoch from all earlier ones. All fixed, fast frozen relations, with their train of ancient and **venerable** prejudices and opinions, are swept away, all new-formed ones become **antiquated** before they can **ossify**. All that is solid melts into air, all that is holy is **profaned**, and man is at last compelled to face with **sober** senses his real condition of life and his relations with his kind.*

The need of a constantly expanding market for its products chases the bourgeoisie over the entire surface of the globe. It must nestle everywhere, settle everywhere, establish connections everywhere....

*The bourgeoisie keeps more and more doing away with the scattered state of the population, of the means of production, and of property. It has **agglomerated** population, centralized the means of production, and has concentrated property in a few hands. The necessary consequence of this was political centralization. Independent, or but loosely connected provinces, with separate interests, laws, governments, and systems of taxation, became lumped together into one nation, with one government, one code of laws, one national class interest, one frontier, and one customs tariff....*

*In proportion as the bourgeoisie, i.e., capital, is developed, in the same proportion is the proletariat, the modern working class, developed—a class of laborers, who live only so long as they find work, and who find work only so long as their labor increases capital. These laborers, who must sell themselves **piecemeal**, are a **commodity**, like every other article of commerce, and are consequently exposed to all the **vicissitudes** of competition, to all the fluctuations of the market.*

*Owing to the extensive use of machinery, and to the division of labor, the work of the proletarians has lost all individual character, and, consequently, all charm for the workman. He becomes an **appendage** of the machine, and it is only the most simple, most*

Exoduses: Departures.

Venerable: Wise.

Antiquated: Outdated.

Ossify: Become rigid

Profaned: Made unholy.

Sober: Serious.

Agglomerated: Gathered into a mass.

Piecemeal: As in by the hour.

Commodity: Something that can be bought and sold.

Vicissitudes: Ups and downs.

Appendage: Part.

Industrial Revolution: Primary Sources

monotonous, and most easily acquired knack, that is required of him. Hence, the cost of production of a workman is restricted, almost entirely, to the means of **subsistence** that he requires for maintenance, and for the **propagation** of his race. But the price of a commodity, and therefore also of labor, is equal to its cost of production. In proportion, therefore, as the repulsiveness of the work increases, the wage decreases. What is more, in proportion as the use of machinery and division of labor increases, in the same proportion the burden of toil also increases, whether by prolongation of the working hours, by the increase of the work exacted in a given time, or by increased speed of machinery, etc.

Modern Industry has converted the little workshop of the **patriarchal** master into the great factory of the industrial **capitalist**. Masses of laborers, crowded into the factory, are organized like soldiers. As privates of the industrial army, they are placed under the command of a perfect **hierarchy** of officers and sergeants. Not only are they slaves of the bourgeois class, and of the bourgeois state; they are daily and hourly enslaved by the machine, by the overlooker, and, above all, by the individual bourgeois manufacturer himself. The more openly this **despotism** proclaims gain to be its end and aim, the more petty, the more hateful and the more embittering it is.

The less the skill and exertion of strength implied in manual labor, in other words, the more modern industry becomes developed, the more is the labor of men **superseded** by that of women. Differences of age and sex have no longer any distinctive social validity for the working class. All are instruments of labor, more or less expensive to use, according to their age and sex.

No sooner is the exploitation of the laborer by the manufacturer, so far at an end, that he receives his wages in cash, than he is set upon by the other portion of the bourgeoisie, the landlord, the shopkeeper, the pawnbroker, etc....

But with the development of industry, the proletariat not only increases in number; it becomes concentrated in greater masses, its strength grows, and it feels that strength more. The various interests and conditions of life within the ranks of the proletariat are more and more equalized, in proportion as machinery **obliterates** all distinctions of labor, and nearly everywhere reduces wages to the same low level. The growing competition among the bourgeois, and the resulting commercial crises, make the wages of the workers ever more fluctuating. The increasing improvement of machinery, ever

Subsistence: Living.

Propagation: Reproduction.

Patriarchical: Fatherly.

Capitalist: One who invests a large amount of money in a business.

Hierarchy: Ranking.

Despotism: Dictatorship.

Superseded: Taken over.

Obliterates: Erases.

more rapidly developing, makes their livelihood more and more **precarious**; the collisions between individual workmen and individual bourgeois take more and more the character of collisions between two classes. Thereupon, the workers begin to form combinations [trade unions] against the bourgeois; they club together in order to keep up the rate of wages; they found permanent associations in order to make provision beforehand for these occasional revolts. Here and there, the contest breaks out into riots....

Of all the classes that stand face to face with the bourgeoisie today, the proletariat alone is a genuinely revolutionary class. The other classes decay and finally disappear in the face of Modern Industry; the proletariat is its special and essential product.

The lower middle class, the small manufacturer, the shopkeeper, the **artisan**, the peasant, all these fight against the bourgeoisie, to save from extinction their existence as fractions of the middle class. They are therefore not revolutionary, but conservative. Nay, more, they are reactionary, for they try to roll back the wheel of history. If, by chance, they are revolutionary, they are only so in view of their impending transfer into the proletariat; they thus defend not their present, but their future interests; they desert their own standpoint to place themselves at that of the proletariat....

In the condition of the proletariat, those of old society at large are already virtually swamped. The proletarian is without property; his relation to his wife and children has no longer anything in common with the bourgeois family relations; modern industry labor, modern subjection to capital, the same in England as in France, in America as in Germany, has stripped him of every trace of national character. Law, morality, religion, are to him so many bourgeois prejudices, behind which lurk in ambush just as many bourgeois interests....

In what relation do the Communists stand to the proletarians as a whole? The Communists do not form a separate party opposed to the other working-class parties.

They have no interests separate and apart from those of the proletariat as a whole.

They do not set up any **sectarian** principles of their own, by which to shape and mold the proletarian movement.

The Communists are distinguished from the other working-class parties by this only:

Precarious: Fragile.

Artisan: Craftsman.

Sectarian: Narrow.

1. In the national struggles of the proletarians of the different countries, they point out and bring to the front the common interests of the entire proletariat, independently of all nationality.

2. In the various stages of development which the struggle of the working class against the bourgeoisie has to pass through, they always and everywhere represent the interests of the movement as a whole....

The distinguishing feature of communism is not the **abolition** of property generally, but the abolition of bourgeois property. But modern bourgeois private property is the final and most complete expression of the system of producing and appropriating products that is based on class antagonisms, on the exploitation of the many by the few.

In this sense, the theory of the Communists may be summed up in the single sentence: Abolition of private property.

Abolition: Officially ending a law, regulation, or practice.

What happened next ...

- The revolutions of 1848 did not succeed in overturning traditional political and economic systems; established authorities restored order. This did not deter Karl Marx and his English colleague and coauthor Friedrich Engels (1820–1895). Marx went on to write *Capital*, published in 1867, which was his analysis of how modern economics works, an answer to Adam Smith's *The Wealth of Nations* (1776; see entry). Marx's writing continued to inspire revolutionaries for decades, and his theories were embraced by the Communist Party of Russia, which seized power in 1917 and formed the Soviet Union.

- Marx thought that history followed an inevitable path, and he predicted in *The Communist Manifesto* that everyone who was not a wealthy owner of factories would join the working class (the proletariat) until there was a violent revolution. In fact, within twenty years of the publication of *The Communist Manifesto,* the political picture in Europe had changed dramatically. Political parties based on the working class had begun to achieve results in reigning in some of the worst abuses of factory owners without a violent revolution. Their movement, called "social democracy," achieved widespread political power throughout Europe in the twentieth century. The "inevitable" revolution predicted by Marx did not come to pass, except in the Soviet Union in 1917, and there under circumstances very different than those envisioned by Marx.

- Even after the collapse of the Soviet Union, and the late-twentieth-century decision by China's leaders to encourage private business owners, the figure of Karl Marx remains revered by hundreds of thousands around the world. Many others revile him as a prophet of evil, particularly for his criticism of religion and its role in society. The *idea* of Marxism remained a powerful force a century and a half after *The Communist Manifesto* was published.

Did you know . . .

As a person, Karl Marx was impatient and sometimes disagreeable. He alienated people with his sarcastic wit and blunt way of speaking. But at the same time, he was a devoted family man. He married his childhood sweetheart, and the couple had seven children, of whom four died as infants or children. Marx was devoted to his children. Of his surviving children (all three of whom were daughters), two married French Socialist politicians who became members of Parliament. His third surviving daughter married a British labor organizer.

For more information

Books

Berlin, Isaiah, Sir. *Karl Marx: His Life and Environment.* 4th ed. New York and Oxford, U.K.: Oxford University Press, 1978.

Eagleton, Terry. *Marx.* New York: Routledge, 1999.

Marx, Karl. *Capital: The Communist Manifesto and Other Writings* (includes translation of *The Communist Manifesto* from German into English by Helen Macfarlane published in *The Red Republican*, June–November 1850). New York: Carlton House, 1932.

Pipes, Richard. *Communism: A History.* New York: Modern Library, 2001.

Andrew Carnegie

Excerpt from "Wealth"

First published in the *North American Review,* June 1889

"In bestowing charity, the main consideration should be to help those who will help themselves."

Andrew Carnegie (1835–1919) was an outstanding symbol of the American dream: a poor immigrant who works hard and achieves astounding success and enormous riches. Carnegie had started on his path to success as a boy, working for low wages in a textile mill, and rose to dominate the steel industry.

At the same time that Carnegie was amassing his fortune, however, more typical immigrants were housed in squalid quarters, earning barely enough to live on. They worked for ten or twelve hours a day, six days a week; they received no vacations and were subject to dismissal at the whim of a supervisor.

In the 1880s the Socialist Party began appealing to such workers to back a profound change. The socialists (people who seek political and economic equality for all people) and other groups, such as the communists (people who believe in a government in which the people own property in common), advocated higher wages and other benefits for workers, which would come at the expense of wealthy owners like Andrew Carnegie. Consequently, Carnegie wrote an essay which he titled simply "Wealth."

Things to remember while reading the excerpt from "Wealth":

- The subject of Carnegie's essay was not an abstract idea for him. In the essay he defends having a huge treasure even while his workers were barely able to live on their wages, and he argues against those who proposed political changes to make the distribution of wealth more even. He argued that it was an inevitable law of history that civilization should advance in such a way as to create a small class of business owners with far greater wealth than ordinary workers. Efforts to change this, as proposed by socialists, communists, and anarchists (people who advocated an end to formal government structures), were doomed to failure—because they went against the natural trends of history, according to Carnegie.

- As part of his justification for accumulating a large fortune, Carnegie also advocated that wealthy individuals should give away their money during their lifetimes in order to benefit society. He was especially intent that such gifts seldom be given directly to individuals in need (as charity), which in his view would simply lead poor people to spend money in a wasteful manner. Rather he believed the money should go to institutions that would improve people's lives. Carnegie himself chose to give money to build public libraries, providing funding to establish libraries in almost every state, and overseas as well.

- In Andrew Carnegie's time, there was no federal tax on incomes (the first federal income tax was imposed after adoption of the Sixteenth Amendment in 1913). Nor was there a federal tax on estates (the property and possessions, including money, left by a person at death). These two facts made it relatively easy for the owners of large corporations of the era to acquire immense fortunes.

- In contrast to a climate favoring the wealthy, there was an almost complete absence of government benefits for workers. If workers were fired or laid off, they were on their own—there was no unemployment assistance to help them until they found another job. Often, workers lived in housing provided by their employer, so that losing a job also meant losing a place to live.

Excerpt from "Wealth"

*The problem of our age is the proper administration of wealth, so that the ties of brotherhood may still bind together the rich and poor in **harmonious** relationship. The conditions of human life have not only been changed, but revolutionized, within the past few hundred years. In former days there was little difference between the dwelling, dress, food, and environment of the chief and those of his **retainers**. The Indians are to-day where civilized man then was. When visiting the **Sioux**, I was led to the **wigwam** of the chief. It was just like the others in external appearance, and even within the difference was **trifling** between it and those of the poorest of his braves. The contrast between the palace of the millionaire and the cottage of the laborer with us to-day measures the change which has come with civilization.*

*This change, however, is not to be **deplored**, but welcomed as highly beneficial. It is well, nay, essential for the progress of the race, that the houses of some should be homes for all that is highest and best in literature and the arts, and for all the **refinements** of civilization, rather than that none should be so. Much better this great irregularity than universal **squalor**. Without wealth there can be no Maecenas [an ancient Roman patron of literature]. The "good old times" were not good old times. Neither master nor servant was as well situated then as to-day. A **relapse** to old conditions would be disastrous to both—not the least so to him who serves—and would sweep away civilization with it. But whether the change be for good or ill, it is upon us, beyond our power to alter, and therefore to be accepted and made the best of. It is waste of time to criticize the inevitable.*

*It is easy to see how the change has come. One illustration will serve for almost every phase of the cause. In the manufacture of products we have the whole story. It applies to all combinations of human industry, as stimulated and enlarged by the inventions of this scientific age. Formerly articles were manufactured at the domestic hearth or in small shops which formed part of the household. The master and his **apprentices** worked side by side, the latter living with the master, and therefore subject to the same conditions. When these apprentices rose to be masters, there was little or no change in their mode of life, and they, in turn, educated in the same*

Harmonious: Agreeable; tranquil.

Retainers: Followers.

Sioux: American Indian tribe.

Wigwam: American Indian hut.

Trifling: Bothering.

Deplored: Condemned.

Refinements: Improvements.

Squalor: Filth; disrepair.

Relapse: Falling back.

Apprentices: Assistants.

routine succeeding apprentices. There was, substantially, social equality, and even political equality, for those engaged in industrial pursuits had then little or no political voice in the State.

But the inevitable result of such a mode of manufacture was crude articles at high prices. To-day the world obtains commodities of excellent quality at prices which even the generation preceding this would have deemed incredible. In the commercial world similar causes have produced similar results, and the race is benefited thereby. The poor enjoy what the rich could not before afford. What were the luxuries have become the necessaries of life. The laborer has now more comforts than the farmer had a few generations ago. The farmer has more luxuries than the landlord had, and is more richly clad and better housed. The landlord has books and pictures rarer, and appointments more artistic, than the King could then obtain.

Andrew Carnegie is depicted in this cartoon as a captain of industry and philanthropy. *Reproduced by permission of Corbis.*

The price we pay for this **salutary** change is, no doubt, great. We assemble thousands of operatives in the factory, in the mine, and in the **counting-house**, of whom the employer can know little or nothing, and to whom the employer is little better than a myth. All **intercourse** between them is at an end. Rigid **Castes** are formed, and, as usual, mutual ignorance breeds mutual distrust. Each Caste is without sympathy for the other, and ready to credit anything **disparaging** in regard to it. Under the law of competition, the employer of thousands is forced into the strictest economies, among which the rates paid to labor figure prominently, and often there is friction between the employer and the employed, between **capital** and labor, between rich and poor. Human society loses **homogeneity**.

The price which society pays for the law of competition, like the price it pays for cheap comforts and luxuries, is also great; but the advantages of this law are also greater still, for it is to this law that we owe our wonderful material development, which brings im-

Salutary: Beneficial.

Counting-house: Office used for bookkeeping.

Intercourse: Social exchanges.

Castes: Groups based on hierarchy.

Disparaging: Insulting.

Capital: Money; resources.

Homogeneity: Being the same throughout.

*proved conditions in its train. But, whether the law be **benign** or not, we must say of it, as we say of the change in the conditions of men to which we have referred: It is here; we cannot evade it; no substitutes for it have been found; and while the law may be sometimes hard for the individual, it is best for the race, because it insures the survival of the fittest in every department. We accept and welcome, therefore, as conditions to which we must accommodate ourselves, great inequality of environment, the concentration of business, industrial and commercial, in the hands of a few, and the law of competition between these, as being not only beneficial, but essential for the future progress of the race. Having accepted these, it follows that there must be great scope for the exercise of special ability in the merchant and in the manufacturer who has to conduct affairs upon a great scale. That this talent for organization and management is rare among men is proved by the fact that it invariably secures for its possessor enormous rewards, no matter where or under what laws or conditions. The experienced in affairs always rate the man whose services can be obtained as a partner as not only the first consideration, but such as to render the question of his capital scarcely worth considering, for such men soon create capital; while, without the special talent required, capital soon takes wings. Such men become interested in firms or corporations using millions; and estimating only simple interest to be made upon the capital invested, it is inevitable that their income must exceed their expenditures, and that they must accumulate wealth. Nor is there any middle ground which such men can occupy, because the great manufacturing or commercial concern which does not earn at least interest upon its capital soon becomes bankrupt. It must either go forward or fall behind: to stand still is impossible. It is a condition essential for its successful operation that it should be thus far profitable, and even that, in addition to interest on capital, it should make profit. It is a law, as certain as any of the others named, that men possessed of this peculiar talent for affairs, under the free play of economic forces, must, of necessity, soon be in receipt of more revenue than can be **judiciously** expended upon themselves; and this law is as beneficial for the race as the others.*

*Objections to the foundations upon which society is based are not in order, because the condition of the race is better with these than it has been with any others which have been tried. Of the effect of any new substitutes proposed we cannot be sure. The **Socialist** or **Anarchist** who seeks to overturn present conditions is to be regarded as attacking the foundation upon which civilization itself*

Benign: Kind.

Judiciously: Wisely.

Socialist: A person who believes in socialism, the political and economic freedom of all people.

Anarchist: A person who advocates rebellion against the ruling power.

rests, for civilization took its start from the day that the capable, industrious workman said to his incompetent and lazy fellow, "If thou dost not sow, thou shalt not reap," and thus ended primitive **Communism** by separating the **drones** from the bees [workers]. One who studies this subject will soon be brought face to face with the conclusion that upon the sacredness of property civilization itself depends—the right of the laborer to his hundred dollars in the savings bank, and equally the legal right of the millionaire to his millions. To those who propose to substitute Communism for this intense Individualism the answer, therefore, is: The race has tried that. All progress from that **barbarous** day to the present time has resulted from its displacement. Not evil, but good, has come to the race from the accumulation of wealth by those who have the ability and energy that produce it. But even if we admit for a moment that it might be better for the race to discard its present foundation, Individualism,—that it is a nobler ideal that man should labor, not for himself alone, but in and for a brotherhood of his fellows, and share with them all in common, realizing **Swedenborg's** idea of Heaven,

Carnegie Hall in New York City is one of many examples of Andrew Carnegie's efforts to use his wealth for the betterment of society at large. *Reproduced by permission of Archive Photos.*

Communism: Form of government in which all the people own property (land and capital) in common.

Drones: Those that live on the labor of others.

Barbarous: Uncivilized.

Swedenborg: Emanuel Swedenborg (1688–1772); Swedish scientist.

where, as he says, the angels derive their happiness, not from laboring for self, but for each other,—even admit all this, and a sufficient answer is, This is not **evolution**, but revolution. It necessitates the changing of human nature itself—a work of **eons**, even if it were good to change it, which we cannot know. It is not practicable in our day or in our age. Even if desirable theoretically, it belongs to another and long-succeeding sociological **stratum**. Our duty is with what is practicable now; with the next step possible in our day and generation. It is criminal to waste our energies in endeavoring to uproot, when all we can profitably or possibly accomplish is to bend the universal tree of humanity a little in the direction most favorable to the production of good fruit under existing circumstances. We might as well urge the destruction of the highest existing type of man because he failed to reach our ideal as to favor the destruction of Individualism, Private Property, the Law of Accumulation of Wealth, and the Law of Competition; for these are the highest results of human experience, the soil in which society so far has produced the best fruit. Unequally or unjustly, perhaps, as these laws sometimes operate, and imperfect as they appear to the **Idealist**, they are, nevertheless, like the highest type of man, the best and most valuable of all that humanity has yet accomplished....

There remains, then, only one mode of using great fortunes; but in this we have the true **antidote** for the temporary unequal distribution of wealth, the **reconciliation** of the rich and the poor—a reign of harmony—another ideal, differing, indeed, from that of the Communist in requiring only the further evolution of existing conditions, not the total overthrow of our civilization. It is founded upon the present most intense individualism, and the race is prepared to put it in practice by degrees whenever it pleases. Under its sway we shall have an ideal state, in which the surplus wealth of the few will become, in the best sense, the property of the many, because administered for the common good, and this wealth, passing through the hands of the few, can be made a much more potent force for the elevation of our race than if it had been distributed in small sums to the people themselves. Even the poorest can be made to see this, and to agree that great sums gathered by some of their fellow-citizens and spent for public purposes, from which the masses reap the principal benefit, are more valuable to them than if scattered among them through the course of many years in trifling amounts....

Poor and restricted are our opportunities in this life; narrow our horizon; our best work most imperfect; but rich men should be

Evolution: Process of change.

Eons: An immeasurable long period of time.

Stratum: Level of society.

Idealist: A visionary.

Antidote: Cure.

Reconciliation: Bringing together of.

thankful for one inestimable **boon**. They have it in their power during their lives to busy themselves in organizing **benefactions** from which the masses of their fellows will derive lasting advantage, and thus dignify their own lives....

This, then, is held to be the duty of the man of Wealth: First, to set an example of modest, **unostentatious** living, shunning display or extravagance; to provide moderately for the legitimate wants of those dependent upon him; and after doing so to consider all surplus revenues which come to him simply as trust funds, which he is called upon to administer, and strictly bound as a matter of duty to administer in the manner which, in his judgment, is best calculated to produce the most beneficial results for the community—the man of wealth thus becoming the mere agent and trustee for his poorer brethren, bringing to their service his superior wisdom, experience, and ability to administer, doing for them better than they would or could do for themselves....

The best uses to which surplus wealth can be put have already been indicated. Those who would administer wisely must, indeed, be wise, for one of the serious obstacles to the improvement of our race is **indiscriminate** charity. It were better for mankind that the millions of the rich were thrown into the sea than so spent as to encourage the slothful, the drunken, the unworthy. Of every thousand dollars spent in so called charity to-day, it is probable that $950 is unwisely spent; so spent, indeed, as to produce the very evils which it proposes to **mitigate** or cure....

In bestowing charity, the main consideration should be to help those who will help themselves; to provide part of the means by which those who desire to improve may do so; to give those who desire to rise the aids by which they may rise; to assist, but rarely or never to do all. Neither the individual nor the race is improved by **alms-giving**. Those worthy of assistance, except in rare cases, seldom require assistance. The really valuable men of the race never do, except in cases of accident or sudden change. Every one has, of course, cases of individuals brought to his own knowledge where temporary assistance can do genuine good, and these he will not overlook. But the amount which can be wisely given by the individual for individuals is necessarily limited by his lack of knowledge of the circumstances connected with each. He is the only true reformer who is as careful and as anxious not to aid the unworthy as he is to aid the worthy, and, perhaps, even more so, for in alms-giving more injury is probably done by rewarding vice than by relieving virtue....

Boon: Benefit.

Benefactions: Good deeds; donations.

Unostentatious: Plain.

Indiscriminate: Without thought or plan.

Mitigate: Ease.

Alms-giving: Donating.

*Thus is the problem of Rich and Poor to be solved. The laws of accumulation will be left free; the laws of distribution free. Individualism will continue, but the millionaire will be but a trustee for the poor; intrusted for a season with a great part of the increased wealth of the community, but administering it for the community far better than it could or would have done for itself. The best minds will thus have reached a stage in the development of the race in which it is clearly seen that there is no mode of disposing of surplus wealth creditable to thoughtful and earnest men into whose hands it flows save by using it year by year for the general good. This day already dawns. But a little while, and although, without incurring the pity of their fellows, men may die sharers in great business enterprises from which their capital cannot be or has not been withdrawn, and is left chiefly at death for public uses, yet the man who dies leaving behind him millions of available wealth, which was his to administer during life, will pass away "unwept, unhonored, and unsung," no matter to what uses he leaves the **dross** which he cannot take with him. Of such as these the public verdict will then be: "The man who dies thus rich dies disgraced."*

*Such, in my opinion, is the true **Gospel** concerning Wealth, obedience to which is destined some day to solve the problem of the Rich and the Poor, and to bring "Peace on earth, among men Good-Will."*

Dross: Something that is worthless.

Gospel: Absolute truth.

What happened next ...

At age sixty-five, Andrew Carnegie had a fortune valued at about $360 million (the equivalent of about $8 billion in 2003). Taking his own advice, Carnegie started giving it away to the sort of institutions described in "Wealth."

As mentioned, he is best remembered for funding public libraries. Every state (except Rhode Island) has at least one public library funded by Andrew Carnegie. He also paid for almost five thousand organs for use in churches around the United States as well as in other countries.

Andrew Carnegie also established pension funds to benefit steelworkers and college professors. Another fund,

Andrew Carnegie helped found Carnegie-Mellon University in Pittsburgh, Pennsylvania, where these students were part of the first group of graduates in a master's degree program in electronic commerce.
Reproduced by permission of AP/Wide World Photos.

the Hero Fund, gave prizes for acts of heroism. In New York City, Carnegie Hall became a renowned auditorium for concerts. Pittsburgh's Carnegie Institute of Technology became a famous college. Carnegie also gave money to many other colleges, including the Tuskegee Institute in Alabama for African Americans.

Still, upon his death, Andrew Carnegie had not succeeded in giving away all his money, as he once advocated. His estate was valued at $23 million (equivalent to about $245 million in 2003) at his death in 1919.

In the meantime, laws were passed designed to address the huge gap in income between business owners and workers. A federal income tax was imposed in 1913, originally paid primarily only by very wealthy citizens, and in 1916 a federal tax on estates was passed. At the same time, government programs were established to provide money for people who lose their jobs. Carnegie probably would have opposed modern welfare payments, insisting that people who cannot find work need to be educated or trained in order to get jobs. It is an argument that has continued since Carnegie's time.

Did you know ...

In 1900 Carnegie Steel was the largest corporation in the world. The next year, Andrew Carnegie sold his company to the financier J. P. Morgan (1837–1913) for $480 million (equivalent to about $5.1 billion in 2003). Morgan said later he would gladly have paid more. Morgan used Carnegie's company as the core of a new company: U.S. Steel.

For more information

Books

Bobinski, George S. *Carnegie Libraries: Their History and Impact on American Public Library Development.* Chicago: American Library Association, 1969.

Carnegie, Andrew. *Autobiography of Andrew Carnegie.* Boston and New York: Houghton Mifflin, 1920.

Carnegie, Andrew. *The Gospel of Wealth, and Other Timely Essays* (includes "Wealth," published in the *North American Review,* June 1889). New York: Century, 1900.

Hacker, Louis Morton. *The World of Andrew Carnegie: 1865–1901.* Philadelphia: Lippincott, 1968.

Livesay, Harold C. *Andrew Carnegie and the Rise of Big Business.* Boston: Little, Brown, 1975.

Web Sites

Carnegie, Andrew. "Wealth." *Furman University's Nineteenth Century Documents and Editorials.* http://www.furman.edu/~benson/docs/carnegie.htm (accessed on April 11, 2003).

Technological Advances and Criticisms

2

Ｎew machines driven by steam and water sparked the Industrial Revolution by substituting mechanical power for human and animal muscles. This was one of the biggest changes in society since human beings started raising crops for food instead of chasing wild game tens of thousands of years earlier.

Many machines were developed to solve specific problems. Pumping water from a coal mine was the problem Thomas Savery (c. 1650–1715) was addressing when he applied in 1798 for a patent on a device he called "the Miner's Friend"—the predecessor of the steam engine. Savery's device used steam to fill a chamber completely, pushing out the air and water; he then cooled the steam quickly, causing it to condense and leave a vacuum, which in turn sucked water from mines. Savery thought, however, that the power of steam could be used in many other ways; he was proven right about fifty years later when another inventor, James Watt (1736–1819), developed the first modern form of the steam engine.

New communications and transportation systems also played an important role in the expansion of the Industrial Revolution. They made it possible to ship raw materials and manufactured goods over long distances economically, and to conduct commerce across the North American continent almost instantaneously. The development of the telegraph by Samuel F. B. Morse (1791–1872) in the United States, and the completion of the transcontinental railroad described by J. D. B. Stillman (1819–1888) linking the East Coast with the Pacific, were seen at the time as exciting developments that could change life. And indeed they did.

On the other hand, technology was viewed as a threat by some people, especially those workers whose jobs were eliminated by the introduction of new machines. In some cases, such as the Luddites and workers of Leeds in England (and as portrayed in the Charlotte Brontë novel, *Shirley*), destroying the machines seemed like a way to return to the previous way of working. The Luddites failed and technological progress moved on.

Thomas Savery

Excerpt from **The Miner's Friend; or,
An Engine to Raise Water by Fire**

Published in 1702

Around the year 1700, owners of British coal mines faced a problem common to mines of all types: how to get rid of the water that constantly seeped into the mine and threatened to flood the deep pits. The existing system, using horses and pulleys to lift buckets filled with water, was expensive and slow. As mines were dug deeper, the bucket system could not keep pace. The challenge of keeping mines dry provided the motivation for development of the steam engine, one of the first steps in a long process of introducing mechanical power alongside human and animal muscles to drive machines—a process called the Industrial Revolution.

Removing water from mines had been a problem for several decades when a British military engineer named Thomas Savery (c. 1650–1715) had an idea he called "an engine to raise [pump out] water by fire." Savery's invention was the first practicable steam engine, using the characteristics of steam to accomplish a task (in his case, to pump water).

Savery's invention started with a boiler (like a huge pot) sitting over burning coal. The fire boiled the water, creating steam. Two pipes led from the boiler to cylindrical contain-

"Then I say, such an engine may be made large enough to do the work required in employing eight, ten, fifteen, or twenty horses."

ers (called receivers). A valve (faucet) was opened on one of these pipes to fill a receiver with steam. As soon as it was full of steam, the valve was closed and cold water was thrown onto the receiver, causing the steam to condense. The condensation of the steam created a vacuum in the receiver, which then sucked water up through a second pipe that connected the receiver with the underground water (at the bottom of the mine, for example). As soon as the first receiver was filled with water, the faucet from the boiler was opened again, and the incoming steam pushed the water out of the receiver through a third pipe. The two receivers alternated in being filled with steam, sucking water from below, and being emptied by the incoming steam. The receivers, in effect, took turns sucking water up from a lower level and expelling it when steam was again let in.

In 1698 Savery demonstrated a working model of his invention for the English king, William III, and was granted a patent. (A patent is a government license granting the exclusive use of an idea for several years, so inventors can earn money from their ideas.) The patent was a broad one, giving Savery the exclusive right to the:

> exercise of a new invention by him invented, for raising of water, and occasioning motion to all sorts of mill works, by the important force of fire, which will be of great use for draining mines, serving towns with water, and for the working of all sorts of mills, when they have not the benefit of water nor constant winds; to hold for 14 years; with usual clauses.

Although Savery's engine was able to raise water, it proved impractical for use in coal mines. The vacuum it created was not strong enough to suck water from the bottom of the deepest mines. Another disadvantage was that the design of Savery's engine required two boilers in order to keep it pumping, which in turn made the "fire engine" too large to fit inside deep mines.

Another English inventor, Thomas Newcomen (1663– 1729), developed a more effective steam engine in 1712, and still later, a third inventor, James Watt (1736–1819), improved on Newcomen's invention. Watt's steam engine was the first that came into widespread use outside of mines. Both Newcomen and Watt used the expansive quality of steam to push a piston (a solid cylindrical piece of metal that slides inside a hollow cylinder) back and forth (or up and down), creating mechanical motion to pump water, or to drive wheels by means of a solid rod connected to one end of the moving piston.

The distinguishing characteristic of Thomas Savery was what he did with his invention. Having obtained his patent, he then set about persuading coal mine owners to use his invention. He published a book titled *The Miner's Friend; or, An Engione to Raise Water by Fire* in 1702 in which he laid out the possible uses of his invention and answered possible objections. In one sense, Thomas Savery was as much a salesman as an inventor, demonstrating a principle that was repeated over and over during the course of the Industrial Revolution: The original inventors were not always the ones who made fortunes. Those inventors who achieved fame and fortune found ways to sell their inventions.

Things to remember while reading the excerpt from *The Miner's Friend:*

- In the excerpt given here from *The Miner's Friend,* Thomas Savery lays out the possibility of using his "Fire Engine to create a circular motion to drive a mill, like a waterwheel pushed by a moving stream was used to grind wheat into flour." This application was not used until James Watt developed an improved version of the steam engine about sixty years later, but Savery evidently had a vision of the future possibilities that came to include the railroad locomotive and steam ship.

- Savery was writing about a century before common spelling was adapted in the English language. Some of his language and original spelling looks odd to readers, two hundred years later.

Excerpt from The Miner's Friend, "Of the Uses That This Engine May Be Applied Unto"

It may be supposed that there are few People among us so ignorant, but must necessarily know of what value the Falls of Water are in most Places, as being applicable to mills; which are made after various kinds and forms, according to the different **genius** and abilities of the mill right; for mill work being in manner infinitely diversified; and had I leisure to comment there on, and give you an account, not only of the vast variety that I have seen and heard of; but (when encouraged) what may yet brought to work by steady stream, and the rotation or circular motion of a water-wheel, it would swell these papers to a much larger volume than was at first designed, and frustrate my intended **brevity**. I only just hint this to show what use this Engine may be put to in working of mills, especially where coals are cheap.

I have only this to urge, that water in its fall from any **determinate** height, has simply a force answerable and equal to the force that raises it. So that an engine which will raise as much water as two horses, working together at one time in such a work, can do, and for which there must be constantly kept ten or twelve horses for doing the same [to give the horses turns at resting]. Then I say, such an engine may be made large enough to do the work required in employing eight, ten, fifteen, or twenty horses to be constantly maintained and kept for doing such a work; it will be improper to **stint** or confine its uses and operation in reflect of water-mills.

It may be of great use for palaces, for the nobilities or gentlemens houses. For by a **cistern** on the top of a house, you may with a great deal of ease and little charge, throw what quantity of water you have occasion for to the top of any house; which water in its fall, makes you what forts of fountains you please and supply any room in the house. And it is of excellent use in case of fire, of which more hereafter.

Nothing can be more fit for serving cities, and towns with water, except a **crank-work** by the force of a river. In the composing such sort of engines, I think no person hath excelled the Mr. **George Sorocold**. But where they are forced to use horses, or any other strength, I believe no ingenious person will deny this engine to have the preference in all respects, being of more universal use than any yet discovered or invented.

As for draining **fens** and marshes, **&c.** I suppose I need say no more than this, that that force which will raise great quantities of water a height of above 80 foot, must necessarily deliver a much greater quantity at a lesser height. And that it is much cheaper, and every way easier, especially where coals are water borne, to contin-

Genius: Ideas.

Brevity: Shortness in time.

Determinate: Specific.

Stint: Limit.

Cistern: Water tank.

Crank-work: To perform a task by using a crank.

George Sorocold (1668–1730): An engineer who devised systems to supply homes with running water from nearby rivers.

Fens: Inland marshes.

&c: Et cetera.

ue the discharge of any quantities of water by our engine, than it can be done by any horse engines what so ever.

I believe it may be made very useful to ships, but I dare not meddle with that matter; and leave it to the judgment of those who are the best judges of **maritain** affairs.

For draining of mines and coal pits, the use of the engine will sufficiently recommend it self, in **raising** water so easier and cheap; and I do not doubt, but that in a few year, it will be a means of making our mining trade, which is no small part of the wealth of this kingdom, double, if not triple to what it now is. And if such vast quantities of lead, tin, and coals are now yearly exported, under the difficulties of such an immense charge and pains as the miners, &c. are now at to discharge their water, how much more may be here-after exported, when the charge will be very much lessened by the use of this engine, every way fitted for the use of mines? For the far greater part of our richest mines and coal-pits, are **liable** to two grand inconveniences, and thereby rendered useless; **viz**. The **eruption and excels** of **subterraneous** waters, as not being worth the expense of draining them by the great charge of horses or hand labor. Or secondly, fatal **damps**, by which many are struck blind, lame, or dead in these subterraneous cavities, if the mine is wanting of a due circulation of air. Now both these inconveniencies are natu-rally remedied by the work of this engine of raising water by the **impellant** force of FIRE.

For the water. Be the mine never so deep, each engine working it 60, 70, or 80 foot high by applying or setting the engines one over another, as shall be showed at large hereafter in the following pages, you may by a sufficient number of engines keep the bottom of any mine dry; and when once you know how large your **feeder** or spring is, it is very easy to know what sized engine, or what number of engines will do your business.

The coals used in this engine is of as little value, as the coals com-monly burned on the mouths of the coal-pits are: for an engine of a **three-inch-bore**, or there about, working the water up 60 foot high, requires a fire-place of not above twenty inches deep and about four-teen or fifteen inches wide, which will occasion so small a **consump-tion**, that in a coal-pit it is of no account, as we have experienced. And in all parts of England where there are mines; coals are so cheap, that the charge of them is not to be mentioned when we consider the vast quantity of water raised by the inconsiderable value of the coals used and burnt in so small a furnace. What the quantity of coals used

Maritain: Ocean.

Raising: Pumping out.

Liable: In danger of.

Viz: Namely.

Eruption and excels: Floods.

Subterraneous: Underground.

Damps: Gases.

Impellant: Driving.

Feeder: Source of water.

Three-inch-bore: Three-inch-wide pipes.

Consumption: Use.

*for one engine in a year is, cannot easily be **ascertained**, because of the different nature of the several sorts of coals.*

*As for the cure of damps by this engine, the air **perpetually** crowding into the ash-hole and fire-place, as it is natural for it to do, and with a most **impetuous** force discharge with the smoke at the top of the chimney, the **contiguous** air is successively following it; so that not only all steams or vapors whatsoever, that may or can arise, must naturally force its way through the fire and so be discharged at the top with the smoke. But this motion of the fire will occasion the fresh Air to descend from above, down all the pits, and every where else in the mine, but down the chimney; provided you have a heading drift, or passage from all the shafts, or pits in the same work it matters not; for here will be a perpetual circulation of air, and with that swiftness, as is hardly to be believed. This I have tried, and know to be true; so leave the ingenious miner to his own judgment. Whether when all the air is in a swift motion, that any **stagnation** of air (which has always been **adjudged** the cause of damps) can happen in any pit.*

Ascertained: Determined.

Perpetually: Constantly.

Impetuous: Insistent.

Contiguous: Surrounding.

Stagnation: Lack of circulation.

Adjudged: Thought to be.

What happened next ...

A few years after Savery received his patent, a humble iron worker named Thomas Newcomen, who lived just fifteen miles away from Savery, proposed a slightly different approach. Newcomen created a vacuum quickly by shooting a jet of cold water into the steam chamber (the collector, in Savery's terms), causing the steam to condense very quickly and make a more effective suction. Newcomen's approach was much closer to modern engines—for one thing, it could repeat the process more quickly than Savery's engine—and might rightly be considered the first modern steam engine.

There is some evidence suggesting that Newcomen was acquainted with Thomas Savery (Newcomen may even have done iron work for Savery), and that the two men may have collaborated on Newcomen's improved model.

James Watt developed an improved version of Newcomen's engine after being asked to repair a model. Later, Watt went into partnership with Matthew Boulton

(1728–1809), a successful businessman. Together, Watt and Boulton began manufacturing steam engines under a patent that gave them a market monopoly (exclusive control). Although Watt is sometimes incorrectly referred to as the inventor of the steam engine (his role was to improve on Newcomen's model), it was really his commercial success that gave him a place in the history of the Industrial Revolution.

Most historians date the start of the Industrial Revolution to around 1750, with the introduction of Watt's successful steam engine. But the steam engine did not begin—or end—with James Watt. It already had a history before Watt was even born.

Did you know ...

The term horsepower was first used by Thomas Savery to describe the power of his steam engine, calculating the number of horses his machine could replace in pulling water up from the bottom of a mine.

For more information

Books

Carnegie, Andrew. *James Watt*. Garden City, NY: Doubleday, Doran, 1933.

Dickinson, H. W. *A Short History of the Steam Engine*. New York: Augustus M. Kelley, 1965.

Hills, Richard L. *Power from Steam: A History of the Stationary Steam Engine*. Cambridge, U.K., and New York: Cambridge University Press, 1989.

Web Sites

Carnegie, Andrew. "James Watt." *University of Rochester: Steam Engine Library*. http://.cif.rochester.edu/~sids/ (accessed on April 10, 2003).

Savery, Thomas. *The Miner's Friend; or, An Engine to Raise Water by Fire*. 1702. Available at *University of Rochester: Steam Engine Library*. http://www.history.rochester.edu/steam/savery (accessed on April 10, 2003).

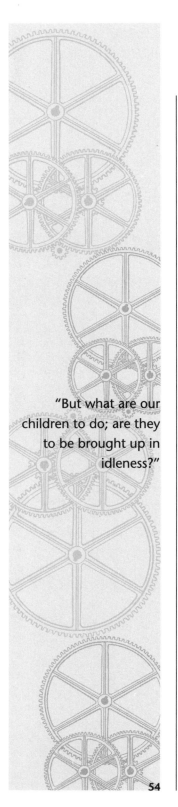

The Workers and Merchants of Leeds

"Yorkshire Cloth Workers' Petition"

Published in the *Leeds Intelligencer* and *Leeds Mercury*, June 13, 1786

"Leeds Cloth Merchant Proclamation in Support of Machinery"

Published in the *Leeds Intelligencer* and *Leeds Mercury*, 1791

"But what are our children to do; are they to be brought up in idleness?"

The move by textile workers from home-based workshops into large factories was the first big social change brought about by the introduction of new machinery into the industry—part of the process known as the Industrial Revolution. Previously, skilled workers spun yarn from cotton or wool and wove it into fabric on smaller machines located in their houses; textiles were called a cottage industry for this reason. But newly invented machines could produce as much yarn or cloth as several individuals using old equipment. These machines, by virtue of their size and expense, were housed in factories, where the formerly independent tradespeople became employees of the factory owners.

This new so-called factory system made a big change in the relationship between a worker and the work. People operating the machines were paid on the basis of how long they worked, instead of on the basis of how much yarn they spun or how much fabric they wove. Instead of supervising themselves, they had to adhere to rules set by the factory owner governing when they would start work and when they could stop for the day. Children as well as adults worked in

factories, and supervisors insisted on strict discipline to keep the machines working continuously and for as many hours a day as possible. Employees often worked up to twelve hours a day with a short break for a meal in the middle.

By 1786 the emerging industrial system was already resulting in complaints from workers who were not used to being supervised when they had worked at home. More important, the workers complained that because the machines could produce so much more yarn or wool in a day, many people who formerly worked at home could no longer find work. They asked what would happen to them and their families if newer machines kept being introduced, causing more jobs to disappear. Their letter (which appears on pages 57–59) is a plea to stop the introduction of machines and stick to the old ways.

The city of Leeds, in the north of England, had become a center of new factories, which is how workers came to publish their petition there in 1786, in the local newspa-

Workers are depicted leaving a textile mill. As advances in technology began to automate the production of goods, many workers worried about being replaced by machines. *Reproduced by permission of Getty Images.*

pers, the *Leeds Intelligencer* and the *Leeds Mercury*. Five years later, in 1791, cloth merchants, who sold fabric both in England and overseas, published their opposing views (which appears on pages 59–61) in the same newspapers. The two statements coming at around the same period are a clear indication of how different the Industrial Revolution appeared to people, depending on whether they had the viewpoint of a worker or of a business owner.

Things to remember while reading the statements of the workers and merchants of Leeds:

- In their petition, which takes the form of a letter addressed to factory owners, the workers argue that new machines in the textile industry had resulted in many people losing their jobs. In many cases, these workers had been trained since childhood to do skilled work, such as weaving, and had no obvious alternatives for employment. Unlike today, there was no unemployment insurance to protect them when they lost their jobs. The workers' proposed solution was to stop the spread of the machines and, in effect, go back to the old ways, which required more people to turn out the same amount of finished products.

- The factory merchants, in their proclamation nearly five years later, also in the form of a letter, pointed out the advantages of the Industrial Revolution, which eventually made England the most powerful country in the world. The factory owners argued that they needed the new machinery in order to be competitive against other nations in processing raw cotton into yarn and cloth. They reminded their readers that competition was international, and that using machines enabled them to sell fabric for less than their competitors and thereby bring even more business to England. More customers would result in more work and higher wages for factory workers, they argued. Eventually, their argument proved to be correct: England was the world's most efficient manufacturer of textiles in the first part of the nineteenth century and sold its goods widely. But the factory owners' letter overlooked the fact that introducing the new system had resulted in widespread difficulty for workers who lost their jobs and who had not yet benefited from increased orders from abroad.

- These two documents are reproduced in their original printed form. In the late 1700s capitalization, punctuation, and spelling did not conform to the conventions that are followed in the twenty-first century.

"Yorkshire Cloth Workers' Petition"

*To the Merchants, Clothiers and all such as wish well to the **Staple Manufactory** of this Nation.*

The Humble ADDRESS and PETITION of Thousands, who labour in the Cloth Manufactory.

*SHEWETH, That the **Scribbling-Machines** have thrown thousands of your petitioners out of employ, whereby they are brought into great distress, and are not able to **procure a maintenance** for their families, and deprived them of the opportunity of bringing up their children to labour. We have therefore to request, that prejudice and self-interest may be laid aside, and that you may pay that attention to the following facts, which the nature of the case requires.*

The number of Scribbling-Machines extending about seventeen miles south-west of LEEDS, exceed all belief, being no less than one hundred and seventy! and as each machine will do as much work in twelve hours, as ten men can in that time do by hand, (speaking within bounds) and they working night and day, one machine will do as much work in one day as would otherwise employ twenty men.

*As we do not mean to assert any thing but what we can prove to be true, we allow four men to be employed at each machine twelve hours, working night and day, will take eight men in twenty-four hours; so that, upon a moderate computation twelve men are thrown out of employ for every single machine used in scribbling; and as it may be supposed the number of machines in all the other quarters together, nearly equal those in the South-West, full four thousand men are left to shift for a living how they can, and must of course **fall to the Parish**, if not timely relieved. Allowing one boy*

Staple Manufactory: Main industry.

Sheweth: Shown.

Scribbling-machines: New machinery.

Procure a maintenance: Earn a living.

Fall to the Parish: Depend on charity.

to be bound **apprentice** from each family out of work, eight thousand hands are deprived of the opportunity of getting a livelihood.

We therefore hope, that the feelings of humanity will lead those who have it in their power to prevent the use of those machines, to give every discouragement they can to what has a tendency so **prejudicial** to their fellow-creatures.

This is not all; the injury to the Cloth is great, in so much that in **Frizzing**, instead of leaving a **nap** upon the Cloth, the wool is drawn out, and the Cloth is left **thread-bare**.

Many more evils we could **enumerate**, but we would hope, that the sensible part of mankind, who are not **biassed** by interest, must see the dreadful tendency of their continuance; a **depopulation** must be the consequence; trade being then lost, the landed interest will have no other satisfaction but that of being last devoured.

We wish to propose a few queries to those who would plead for the further continuance of these machines:

Men of common sense must know, that so many machines in use, take the work from the hands employed in Scribbling, —and who did that business before machines were invented.

How are those men, thus thrown out of employ to provide for their families; —and what are they to put their children apprentice to, that the rising generation may have something to keep them at work, in order that they may not be like **vagabonds** strolling about in idleness? Some say, Begin and learn some other business. —Suppose we do; who will maintain our families, whilst we undertake the **arduous** task; and when we have learned it, how do we know we shall be any better for all our pains; for by the time we have served our second apprenticeship, another machine may arise, which may take away that business also; so that our families, being **half pined** whilst we are learning how to provide them with bread, will be wholly so during the period of our third apprenticeship.

But what are our children to do; are they to be brought up in idleness? Indeed as things are, it is no wonder to hear of so many executions [for crimes]; for our parts, though we may be thought **illiterate** men, our conceptions are, that bringing children up to industry, and keeping them employed, is the way to keep them from falling into those crimes, which an idle habit naturally leads to.

These things **impartially** considered will we hope, be strong advocates in our favour; and we conceive that men of sense, religion

Apprentice: Assistant to a skilled worker.

Prejudicial: Harmful.

Frizzing: A step in weaving wool cloth.

Nap: Bump of thread.

Thread-bare: Scant.

Enumerate: Number.

Biassed: Leaning to one opinion over another.

Depopulation: Lessening of the number of workers.

Vagabonds: Shiftless individuals.

Arduous: Difficult.

Half pined: Lost their health.

Illiterate: Unable to read or write.

Impartially: Objectively; fairly.

and humanity, will be satisfied of the reasonableness, as well as necessity of this address, and that their own feelings will urge them to **espouse** *the cause of us and our families—*

Signed in behalf of THOUSANDS, by

Joseph Hepworth	*Thomas Lobley*
Robert Wood	*Thos. Blackburn.*

"Leeds Cloth Merchant Proclamation in Support of Machinery"

BEING informed that various Kinds of MACHINERY, for the better and more **expeditious DRESSING** *OF WOOLLEN-CLOTH, have been lately invented, that many such Machines are already made and set to work in different Parts of this County, and that great Numbers more are contracted for, to be used in the Dressing of Cloth in other Parts of Yorkshire, and in the Counties of Lancaster, Derby, Chester, Wilts and Gloucester, thought it necessary to meet together on the Eighteenth of October, to take into their most serious Consideration what Steps were needful to be taken, to prevent the Merchants and Cloth-Dressers in other Parts, from diminishing the* **Staple Trade** *of this Town, by the Enjoyment of superior Implements in their Business.*

At the said Meeting, attended by almost every Merchant in the Town, the above Facts did clearly appear, and after a Discussion of the Merits of various Inventions, and the Improvement in Dressing likely to be derived from them, it appeared to them all, absolutely necessary that this Town should partake of the Benefit of all Sorts of Improvements that are, or can be made in the Dressing of their Cloths, to prevent the Decline of that Business, of which the Town of Leeds has for Ages had the greatest Share, and which from its local Advantages, we presume may be maintained and increased, provided the Merchants, and Dressers of Cloth, in Leeds, do not neglect to use the best Means in their Power, of performing their Work to the utmost Perfection.

In order that the Matter should be undertaken on a Plan to afford every possible Information, a Committee was then appointed for the Purpose of obtaining one of each of the different Machines now in Use, on the most approved Construction, and a Subscription was entered into for **defraying** *the Expence thereof, and to enable them to obtain an eligible Situation for erecting and working them,*

Espouse: Advocate.

Expeditious: Speedy.

Dressing: Preparation.

Staple Trade: Chief business.

Defraying: Paying.

for the Inspection of the Trade, previous to their being brought into general Use.

At a time when the People, engaged in every other Manufacture in the Kingdom, are exerting themselves to bring their Work to Market at reduced Prices, which can alone be effected by the Aid of Machinery, it certainly is not necessary that the Cloth Merchants of Leeds, who depend chiefly on a **Foreign Demand**, where they have for Competitors the Manufacturers of other Nations, whose Taxes are few, and whose manual Labour is only Half the Price it bears here, should have Occasion to defend a Conduct, which has for its Aim the Advantage of the Kingdom in general, and of the Cloth Trade in particular; yet anxious to prevent Misrepresentations, which have usually attended the Introduction of the most useful Machines, they wish to remind the Inhabitants of this Town, of the Advantages derived to every flourishing Manufacture from the Application of Machinery; they instance that of Cotton in particular, which in its internal and foreign Demand is nearly alike to our own, and has in a few Years by the Means of Machinery advanced to its present Importance, and is still increasing.

If then by the Use of Machines, the Manufacture of Cotton, an Article which we import, and are supplied with from other Countries, and which can every where be **procured** on equal Terms, has met with such amazing Success, may not greater Advantages be reasonably expected from cultivating to the utmost the Manufacture of Wool, the Produce of our own Island, an Article in Demand in all Countries, and almost the universal Cloathing of Mankind?

In the Manufacture of Woollens, the Scribbling Mill, the **Spinning Frame**, and the **Fly Shuttle**, have reduced manual Labour nearly One third, and each of them at its first Introduction carried an Alarm to the Work People, yet each has contributed to advance the Wages and to increase the Trade, so that if an Attempt was now made to deprive us of the Use of them, there is no Doubt, but every Person engaged in the Business, would exert himself to defend them.

From these Premises, we the undersigned Merchants, think it a Duty we owe to ourselves, to the Town of Leeds, to the Nation at large, to declare that we will protect and support the free Use of the proposed Improvements in Cloth Dressing, by every legal Means in our Power; and if after all, contrary to our Expectations, the Introduction of Machinery should for a Time occasion a **Scarcity** of Work in the Cloth Dressing Trade, we have unanimously agreed to give a

Foreign Demand: The demand by other countries for goods.

Procured: Acquired.

Spinning Frame: A machine used to manufacture yarn.

Fly Shuttle: A loom that speeded the weaving of cloth.

Scarcity: Shortage.

The development of new machines such as the spinning wheel (pictured) improved productivity but caused worry among laborers, whose way of life changed dramatically. *Reproduced by permission of the Corbis Corporation.*

Preference to such Workmen as are now settled Inhabitants of this Parish, and who give no Opposition to the present Scheme.

[The document closed with the signatures of sixty-one Leeds merchants.]

What happened next ...

Despite the protests of the workers, the process of introducing machines (called industrialization) continued in England without pause. Ten years after the mill owners published their response, some workers tried to slow down the process by vandalizing new factories that they viewed as robbing them of jobs. Led by a character named Ned Ludd (possibly a fictitious person), the so-called Luddites tried to use sabotage as a means of preserving their jobs. The effort failed completely.

The hardships endured by workers eventually resulted in radical political movements, such as socialism and communism, in which workers tried to exert government control over industry, either by passing regulations or by seizing private property. Workers concluded that their interests were different from the interests of factory owners, and they organized labor unions and political movements designed to advance the interests of workers at the expense of factory owners. Eventually their voices were heard, and during the course of the nineteenth century, the governments of Britain and other industrialized countries, including the United States, passed laws limiting the hours that children could work and establishing new safety regulations for factories.

Did you know …

As late as 1803, seventeen years after the textile workers wrote their letter, only about 16 percent of woolen fabric was being produced in a factory in Leeds. Hand-operated looms were still the dominant source of cloth. The introduction of the power loom, in 1820, was a much more significant advancement in the industrialization of the British textile industry than were the machines invented earlier.

For more information

Books

Foster, John. *Class Struggle and the Industrial Revolution: Early Industrial Capitalism in Three English Towns.* New York: St. Martin's Press, 1974.

Harrison, J. F. C. *Society and Politics in England, 1780–1960: A Selection of Readings* (includes "Yorkshire Cloth Workers' Petition" and "Leeds Cloth Merchant Proclamation in Support of Machinery" published in the *Leeds Intelligencer* and *Leads Mercury* in 1786 and 1791). New York: Harper and Row, 1965.

Jennings, Humphrey. *Pandaemonium: The Coming of the Machine as Seen by Contemporary Observers, 1660–1886.* New York: Free Press, 1985.

Mantoux, Paul. *The Industrial Revolution in the Eighteenth Century: An Outline of the Beginnings of the Modern Factory System in England.* Edited by Mary-Lou Jennings and Charles Madge. Translated by Marjorie Vernon. New York: Macmillan, 1961.

The Luddites

Various documents attributed to the Luddites

Delivered in 1811

Charlotte Brontë

Excerpt from Shirley, a Tale

Published in 1849

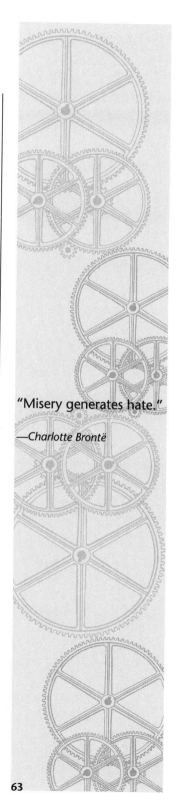

"Misery generates hate."

—*Charlotte Brontë*

The introduction of newly invented water- or steam-powered machinery into England's textile industry, starting in the last quarter of the eighteenth century, had a major impact on workers right from the beginning. People skilled at making yarn or fabric with traditional hand-operated spinning machines or looms soon discovered that with the new equipment, one or two workers could produce the same amount of yarn or cloth as a dozen or more workers using the old machines. With fewer workers needed to produce the same amount of goods, jobs in textiles became harder to find. In 1811 near Nottingham, England, a group of workers who made knee-high stockings that were commonly worn with short trousers (called breeches) reacted to these changes by breaking into factories and wrecking the new machines. The vandals came to be known as "Luddites," a word that has come to mean people who reject technical innovation.

The original Luddites also criticized owners of the new machines for replacing highly skilled workers with people with far less training or experience, even though the machines had taken over some of the skilled tasks needed to make yarn and fabric by hand. (In their letters of protest, the Luddites often referred to the new equipment as "frames," a reference to the fact that fabric looms looked like the outside edges of a hollow box, on which yarn was strung for weaving or knitting. Knitting and weaving are two different techniques for making fabric from yarn.) Unskilled people were willing to work for lower wages than the skilled workers, which resulted in a reduction in wages for everyone in the textile industry.

At first, factory owners ignored the protests. In frustration, some workers turned to violence, destroying the new machines they blamed for their economic problems. The vandals sent letters signed with the name "General Ned Ludd" (or variations of this name, such as Nedd Lud and Edward Ludd). Some historians think Ned Ludd was the name of an actual person, a man of limited intelligence who lived in the area of Leicestershire, England, around 1779. According to a story told about him, after being teased by village boys he chased his tormentors into a house. There, in frustration, he wrecked two machines used for making stockings. Other historians say that Ned Ludd was a real person involved in the antimachine riots. Still others insist that Ned Ludd was a fictitious character, a pseudonym (false name) used to disguise the identity of the letter writers.

What the authors of the Luddite letters had in common was an evidently limited education, which was not surprising since children as young as eight often stopped school and went to work helping their parents spin yarn at home, or later, to operate machines in the newly built factories. The Luddite letters reflect a degree of illiteracy and irregular spelling. In some cases, they are attempts to mimic formal legal documents.

Although the Luddites could not write perfect English, they were well organized. Their attacks on factories were not just random riots; they were planned, and often factory owners received threats in advance.

This collection of documents illustrates several sides of the Luddites. The first document is a threat against a specific owner of new textile machines. It is written to sound like an official document, perhaps the writer's notion of a formal legal indictment (accusation), even though it was doubtless drawn up by workers who had no official standing.

The second document is a Luddite oath. Many of these documents were collected by local officials and sent to the British parliament in London as a warning that trouble was brewing among textile workers. The oath indicates that the Luddites were an organized group that had specific goals, including keeping the names of members a secret.

The third document is from a fragment of a paper that was delivered as a threat against a factory owner. It shows both the intent of the Luddites and the limited education of most workers in the era. (Because it is only a fragment, it contains some breaks that do not make immediate sense.)

The fourth document is a letter from unemployed knitters to hosiery manufacturers in Nottingham, England. It was written early in the Luddite uprising and lays out the complaints of the workers.

The fifth document is a fragment of a follow-up letter, purportedly written by Ned Ludd, one month after the previous letter from the knitters, warning that unless the stocking makers take action, they will have to face the consequences.

The last document is an excerpt from the 1849 novel *Shirley, a Tale,* by Charlotte Brontë (1816–1855). This fictional account, written almost forty years after the attacks by the Luddites, describes a nighttime raid by disaffected workers, and the determination of a factory owner to protect his property. The main characters in the story are Robert Gerard Moore, who owns a textile factory, and Shirley Keeldar, a woman Moore is courting at least partly to gain access to her inherited fortune. The other two characters in this passage are Mr. Malone, a curate (assistant clergyman), and Caroline Helstone, a teenage friend of Shirley Keeldar. In the passage, Moore is waiting for some new machines to be delivered, ready to protect them from an attack by Luddites. Shirley and her friend Caroline are at home, not far from the factory, listening to the sounds of the attack that soon came.

Things to remember while reading various Luddite documents and the excerpt from Charlotte Brontë's *Shirley, a Tale:*

- At the time of the Luddite movement, England was fighting a war against Napoléon Bonaparte (1769–1821), the emperor of France who was intent on spreading French power and influence throughout Europe. This war had a negative effect on the English economy and made the conditions of textile workers even more difficult. The promise of the new machines was to sell more cloth to customers worldwide, but trading opportunities were limited during the war against France. The result was widespread unemployment among textile workers, who blamed their woes on the new machines rather than on the restraints on foreign trade caused by the war with France.

- Britain's war with France made the Luddites seem especially threatening. The French Revolution (1789–99) had advocated equality for all men, whereas political power in England was still limited to property owners. Some people in England saw the Luddites as people who wanted to stage a revolution similar to the French Revolution, and for that reason the government was quick to come down hard on the Luddites, dispatching troops to maintain order.

- Many, or most, textile workers in 1811 did not know how to read or write. This illiteracy is reflected in some of the Luddite documents reproduced here. On the other hand, some of the documents reflect an effort to mimic legal documents, using terms such as whereas, enjoin, adjudge, and forfeited. The original spelling and appearance of the documents has been preserved here.

Luddite letter threatening an owner of textile machines

Declaration; Extraordinary.

Justice.

Death, or Revenge.

To our well-beloved Brother, and Captain in Chief, Edward Ludd.

*Whereas, it **hath** been represented to us: the General Agitators, for the Northern Counties, assembled to **redress** the Grievances of the Operative Mechanics, That Charles Lacy, of the Town of Nottingham,*

Hath: Have.

Redress: Address.

British Lace Manufacturer, has been guilty of **divers fraudulent, and oppressiv,** Acts—whereby he has reduced to poverty and Misery Seven Hundred of our beloved Brethren; moreover, it hath been represented to us that the said Charles Lacy, by making fraudulent Cotton Point Nett, of One Thread Stuff, has obtain^d the Sum of Fifteen Thousand Pounds, whereby he has ruine^d the Cotton-Lace Trade, and consequently our worthy and wellbelov^d Brethren; whose support and comfort depended on the continuance of that manufacture.

It appeareth to us that the said Charles Lacy was **actuated** by the most **diabolical** motives, namely to get rich gain riches by the misery of his Fellow Creatures, we therefore willing to make an example of the said Charles Lacy, do **adjudge** the said Fifteen Thousand Pounds to be **forfeited,** and we do hereby authorise, impower, and enjoin you, to command Charles Lacy to **disburse** the said sum, in equal shares among the Workmen, who made Cotten Nett in the Year 1807, within ten Days from the Date hereof.

In default whereof, we do command that you inflict the Punishment of Death on the said Charles Lacy, and we do authorise you to distribute among the party you may employ for that purpose the Sum of Fifty Pounds, we enjoin you to cause this our Order to be presented to the said Charles Lacy without Delay,

November 1811—By Order Thos Death

A Luddite Oath

I, AB, of my own free will and accord do hereby promise and swear that I will never reveal any of the names of any one of this secret Committee, under the penalty of being sent out of this world by the first Brother that may meet me. I furthermore do swear, that I will pursue with unceasing **vengeance** any Traitors or Traitor, should there any arise, should he fly to the verge of—I furthermore do swear that I will be sober and faithful, in all my dealings with all my Brothers, and if ever I decline them, my name to be blotted out from the list of Society and never to be remembered, but with **contempt** and **abhorrence,** so help me God to keep this our Oath **inviolate.**

Signed Thomas Broughton.

A Luddite threat

M^r H—[illegible]

at Bullwell

Divers Fraudulent, oppresiv: Illegal.

Actuated: Moved into action.

Diabolical: Sinister.

Adjudge: Pronounce.

Forfeited: Gave up rights.

Disburse: Distribute.

Vengeance: Punishment in return for an injury or offense.

Contempt: Act of despising.

Abhorrence: Aversion.

Inviolate: Pure.

S[r],

Sir if you do not pull don the Frames

or stop pay [in] Goods onely for work

extra work or m[ake] in Full fashon

my Companey will [vi]sit y[r] machines

for execution agai[nst] you—

M[r] Bolton the Forfeit—

I visit[d] him—

Ned Lud

Kings [illegible]

An address from the framework knitters to the gentlemen hosiers of the town of Nottingham

Nottingh[m]—Novemb[r] 28 1811

GENTLEMEN,—*At a time like the present, so big with **Calamity** and Distress, we think it right to **solicit** your Advice, Aid, and Direction, as we know no Reason why our Business, which is looked upon as the staple Trade, and principal Support of the Community at large, should be exposed to so many Evils, without any suitable means of defence; or if [there are] any, why [they are] not brought forward into exercise. As we have nothing in view but a reciprocal Advantage in the Trade, both for ourselves and you, and a mutual good Understanding in all our Actions, we solicit your Advice, Aid, Direction, and Support, in this time of our Calamity and Distress, and we think we have a humble Claim upon you for it. On account of the great rise of all the Necessaries of Life, a Man that has full employ, with all his industry, and a Woman, with all her care and economy, can by no means support a Family with any degree of Comfort. If this is the Case (which it really is) how **deplorable** must the situation of those be, that have but a small portion of Employ, and at very low Rates; but still worse, what must the situation of those be that have none at all, which is the Case with **incalculable** numbers at this time. **Destitute** of all the Comforts of Life, our only acquaintance is pinching Poverty and pining Want. We wish to live peaceably and honestly by our Labour, and to train up our Children in the paths of virtue and **rectitude**, but we cannot accomplish our wishes. Our Children, instead of being trained up by a regular course of Education,*

Calamity: State of deep misery caused by major misfortune.

Solicit: To approach with a request or offer.

Deplorable: Deserving to be frowned upon.

Incalculable: Not measurable.

Destitute: Lacking.

Rectitude: Moral strength or integrity.

for social life, virtuous employments, and all the reciprocal advantages of mutual enjoyment, are scarce one remove from the **Brute**, are left to all the dangerous Evils attendant on an uncultivated Mind, and often fall dreadful Victims to that guilt, which Ignorance is the parent of. But, Gentlemen, we **forbear**, as we think it would be insulting both to your judgments and feelings, were we to attempt a description of all our Calamities, which you so well know, and which we so much experience. Our request, Gentlemen, is that you will favor us with your best Advice, respecting as Address to Parliament, for the better Regulation of our Trade, and means of defence against future **Impositions**. Being well assured that the most suitable means lie in the **compass of your breasts**, we wish to pay all **deference** to your superior judgments, and are now waiting for your decision, which we hope you will favor us with as soon as possible; that if it meets your views, the Business may be conducted peaceably and in good order, to our mutual Comfort and Advantage.

Follow-up letter (fragment) allegedly written by Ned Ludd, appearing one month after the above communication

Ned Lud Gives Notic, to the Coperation [Ned Ludd Gives Notice to the Corporation]

if the Coperation does not take means to Call A

Meeting with the **Hoseiars** about the prices Being—

Droped Ned will asemble 20000 Menn together in a few Days

and will Destroy the town in Spite of the Soldiers—

no King—

Excerpt from Charlotte Brontë's Shirley, a Tale

The "**Orders in Council**," provoked by Napoleon's Milan and Berlin decrees, and forbidding neutral powers to trade with France, had, by offending America, cut off the principal market of the Yorkshire woollen trade, and brought it consequently to the verge of ruin. Minor foreign markets were **glutted**, and would receive no more: the Brazils, Portugal, Sicily, were all overstocked by nearly two years' consumption. At this crisis certain inventions in machinery were introduced into the **staple manufactures** of the north, which, greatly reducing the number of hands necessary to be employed,

Brute: Resembling an animal in quality.

Forbear: Refrain or stop.

Impositions: Difficult situations.

Compass of your breasts: Direction of your hearts.

Deference: Respect.

Hoseiars: Hosery makers.

Orders in Council: Resolutions passed in a voting body.

Glutted: Oversupplied.

Staple manufactures: Necessary products.

*threw thousands out of work, and left them without legitimate means of sustaining life. A bad harvest **supervened**. Distress reached its climax. Endurance, **overgoaded**, stretched the hand of fraternity to **sedition**. The throes of a sort of moral earthquake were felt heaving under the hills of the northern counties. But, as is usual in such cases, nobody took much notice. When a food riot broke out in a manufacturing town, when a **gig-mill** was burnt to the ground, or a manufacturer's house was attacked, the furniture thrown into the streets, and the family forced to flee for their lives, some local measures were or were not taken by the local **magistracy**; a ringleader was detected, or more frequently suffered [allowed] to elude detection; newspaper paragraphs were written on the subject, and there the thing stopped. As to the sufferers [workers], whose sole inheritance was labour, and who had lost that inheritance—who could not get work, and consequently could not get wages, and consequently could not get bread—they were left to suffer on; perhaps inevitably left: it would not do to stop the progress of invention, to damage science by discouraging its improvements; the war could not be terminated, efficient relief could not be raised: there was no help then; so the unemployed underwent their destiny—ate the bread and drank the waters of affliction.*

*Misery generates hate: these sufferers hated the machines which they believed took their bread from them: they hated the buildings which contained those machines; they hated the manufacturers who owned those buildings. In the parish of Briarfield, with which we have at present to do, Hollow's Mill was the place held most **abominable**; Gerard Moore, in his double character of **semi-foreigner** and thoroughgoing **progressist**, the man most abominated. And it perhaps rather agreed with Moore's temperament than otherwise to be generally hated especially when he believed the thing for which he was hated a right and an **expedient** thing; and it was with a sense of warlike excitement he, on this night, sat in his **counting-house** waiting the arrival of his frame-laden waggons. Malone's coming and company were, it may be, most unwelcome to him: he would have preferred sitting alone; for he liked a silent, sombre, unsafe solitude: his watchman's **musket** would have been company enough for him....*

"What are they doing now, Shirley? What is that noise?"

"Hatchets and crowbars against the yard-gates: they are forcing them. Are you afraid?"

Supervened: Took place unexpectedly.

Overgoaded: Prompted excessively.

Sedition: Resistance to or insurrection against lawful authority.

Gig-mill: Yarn factory.

Magistracy: Law offices.

Abominable: Horrible.

Semi-foreigner: Not from the same town.

Progressist: Supporter of the common person.

Expedient: Appropriate.

Counting-house: Office used for bookkeeping.

Musket: An early form of rifle.

"No; but my heart throbs fast; I have a difficulty in standing: I will sit down. Do you feel unmoved?"...

"Shirley—Shirley, the gates are down! That crash was like the felling of great trees. Now they are pouring through. They will break down the mill doors as they have broken the gate: what can **Robert** do against so many? Would to God I were a little nearer him—could hear him speak—could speak to him! With my will—my longing to serve him—I could not be a useless burden in his way: I could be turned to some account."

"They come on!" cried Shirley. "How steadily they march in! There is discipline in their ranks—I will not say there is courage: hundreds against tens are no proof of that quality but" (she dropped her voice) "there's suffering and desperation enough amongst them—these **goads** will urge them forwards."

"Forwards against Robert—and they hate him. Shirley, is there much danger they will win the day?..."

A crash—smash—shiver—stopped their whispers. A **simultaneously**-hurled volley of stones had **saluted** the broad front of the mill, with all its windows; and now every pane of every lattice lay shattered and pounded fragments. A yell followed this demonstration—a rioters' yell—a North-of-England—a Yorkshire—a West-Riding—a West-Riding-clothing-district-of Yorkshire rioters' yell. You never heard that sound, perhaps, reader? So much the better for your ears—perhaps for your heart; since, if it rends the air in hate to yourself, or to the men or principles you approve, the interests to which you wish well. **Wrath** wakens to the cry of Hate: the Lion shakes his mane, and rises to the howl of the Hyena: **Caste** stands up **ireful** against Caste; and the **indignant**, wronged spirit of the **Middle Rank** bears down in **zeal** and scorn on the **famished** and furious mass of the **Operative** class. It is difficult to be tolerant—difficult to be just—in such moments.

Caroline rose, Shirley put her arm round her: they stood together as still as the straight stems of two trees. That yell was a long one, and when it ceased, the night was yet full of the swaying and murmuring of a crowd.

"What next?" was the question of the listeners. Nothing came yet. The mill remained mute as a **mausoleum**....

Shots were discharged by the rioters. Had the defenders waited for this signal? It seemed so. The hitherto **inert** and passive mill

Robert: Robert Gerard Moore, a character in the novel.

Goads: Things used to stir someone into action.

Simultaneously: At the same time.

Saluted: Hit.

Wrath: Vengeance.

Caste: Social class.

Ireful: Angry.

Indignant: Angered about something.

Middle Rank: Middle class.

Zeal: Passion.

Famished: Hungry, deprived.

Operative: Engaged in work.

Caroline: Caroline Helstone, a teenage friend of the character Shirley.

Mausoleum: A stone building for entombing the dead above ground.

Inert: Motionless.

woke: fire flashed from its empty window-frames; a volley of **musketry** pealed sharp through the **Hollow**.

"Moore speaks at last!" said Shirley, "and he seems to have the gift of tongues; that was not a single voice."

"He has been forbearing; no one can accuse him of **rashness**," alleged Caroline: "their discharge preceded his: they broke his gates and his windows; they fired at his **garrison** before he repelled them."

What was going on now? It seemed difficult, in the darkness, to distinguish, but something terrible, a still-renewing **tumult**, was obvious: fierce attacks, desperate repulses; the mill-yard, the mill itself, was full of battle movements: there was scarcely any **cessation** now of the discharge of firearms; and there was struggling, rushing, trampling, and shouting between. The aim of the assailants seemed to be to enter the mill, that of the defendants to beat them off. They heard the rebel leader cry, "To the back, lads!" They heard a voice retort, "Come round, we will meet you!"

"To the counting-house!" was the order again.

"Welcome! We shall have you there!" was the response. And accordingly, the fiercest blaze that had yet glowed, the loudest rattle that had yet been heard, burst from the counting-house front, when the mass of rioters rushed up to it....

The rioters had never been so met before. At other mills they had attacked, they had found no resistance; an organised, **resolute** defence was what they never dreamed of encountering. When their leaders saw the steady fire kept up from the mill, witnessed the composure and determination of its owner, heard themselves coolly defied and invited on to death, and beheld their men falling wounded round them, they felt that nothing was to be done here. In **haste**, they **mustered** their forces, drew them away from the building: a roll was called over, in which the men answered to figures instead of names: they dispersed wide over the fields, leaving silence and ruin behind them. The attack, from its commencement to its termination, had not occupied an hour....

The mill **yawned** all ruinous with unglazed frames; the yard was thickly **bestrewn** with stones and **brickbats**, and, close under the mill, with the glittering fragments of the shattered windows, muskets and other weapons lay here and there; more than one deep **crimson** stain was visible on the gravel; a human body lay

Musketry: Gunfire.

Hollow: Valley.

Rashness: Ill-considered haste.

Garrison: A military post.

Tumult: Disorderly commotion or disturbance.

Cessation: A discontinuation.

Resolute: Determined.

Haste: Hurry.

Mustered: Assembled.

Yawned: Opened wide.

Bestrewn: Scattered.

Brickbats: Pieces of broken brick used as weapons.

Crimson: Red, as in blood.

quiet on its face near the gates; and five or six wounded men writhed and moaned in the bloody dust.

Miss [Shirley] Keeldar's countenance changed at this view: it was the after-taste of the battle, death and pain replacing excitement and exertion: it was the blackness the bright fire leaves when its blaze is sunk, its warmth failed, and its glow faded.

What happened next ...

In 1812 the Luddite movement spread to other areas of Britain where new looms had been introduced. The British government was quick to react. In 1812 Parliament passed the Frame Breaking Act, making wrecking of machinery a capital offense, meaning that people convicted of doing so could be executed. Twelve thousand troops were sent to the affected areas to guard factories.

Some factory owners hired armed men to guard their property. In one case, in Yorkshire, at least two Luddites were killed while attacking a factory. A few days later, the owner of another factory was killed. Fourteen workers were hanged for attacking the first factory, and three others were executed for murdering the factory owner in the second case.

Over time, the Luddite movement died out as workers became discouraged. The number of new spinning machines and looms continued to increase, and there was no evidence that wrecking them was going to slow the progress of the Industrial Revolution. The last attack connected with the Luddite movement occurred in 1817.

Did you know ...

The term "Luddite" remains in use today, to describe people opposed to the rapid introduction of new technology, such as computers and the Internet or biotechnology (developing new varieties of grains, for example). Some people have adopted the term "neo-Luddite" (new Luddite) to describe themselves. They argue that new technology should not be adopted without taking into account the costs in disruption of peoples' lives.

On the other hand, some people who call themselves neo-Luddites have embraced technology, arguing that computers linked to the Internet will enable individuals to regain control over their lives, control that was lost when the Industrial Revolution forced many independent workers into factories. The role of technology in society remains a subject of intense debate.

For more information

Bailey, Brian J. *The Luddite Rebellion.* New York: New York University Press, 1998.

Brontë, Charlotte. *Shirley, a Tale.* 1849. Reprint, Edinburgh, Scotland: J. Grant, 1905.

Sale, Kirkpatrick. *Rebels Against the Future: The Luddites and Their War on the Industrial Revolution: Lessons for the Computer Age.* Reading, MA: Addison-Wesley Publishing Co., 1995.

Thomis, Malcolm I. *The Luddites: Machine-Breaking in Regency England.* New York: Schocken Books, 1972.

Web Sites

Binfield, Kevin, ed. "Texts of the Nottinghamshire Luddites" (includes Luddite letter threatening an owner of textile machines, A Luddite threat, An address from the framework knitters to the gentlemen hosiers of the town of Nottingham, and Follow-up letter [fragment] allegedly written by Ned Ludd). *MSU RacerNet.* http://campus.murray state.edu/academic/faculty/kevin.binfield/luddites_sample.htm (accessed on April 10, 2003).

"A Luddite Oath." *A Web of English History.* http://dspace.dial.pipex. com/town/terrace/adw03/c-eight/distress/oath.htm (accessed on April 10, 2003).

Newpaper Accounts Regarding the Telegraph

Articles published in the New York Herald *and an untitled article from an unknown source*

Published in 1844 and 1848

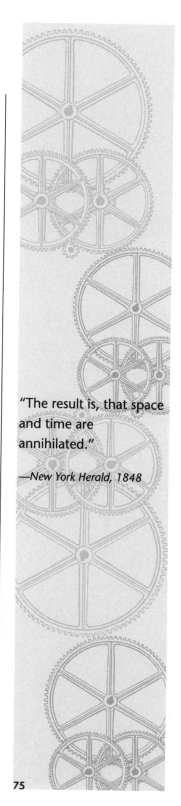

I t is hard to imagine the world of 1842, when Samuel F. B. Morse (1791–1872) was struggling to make a success of his invention, the electric telegraph.

Electric lights for reading this book? Not invented yet.

Utility poles carrying telephone, electric, and cable TV wires? Nonexistent.

News received minutes after it happens (or even as it's happening, via television)? Unimaginable.

Until 1844 long-distance communication in the United States relied on the U.S. Post Office, and even then letters were only delivered to towns and cities, not to the farms where millions of Americans lived at the time. Letters and news took days, or weeks, to arrive. Newspapers received copies of other papers from big cities, and reprinted stories days later. It was dramatically different from the world of the Internet and the World Wide Web, in which news from every part of the world is delivered in a matter of seconds.

"The result is, that space and time are annihilated."

—*New York Herald, 1848*

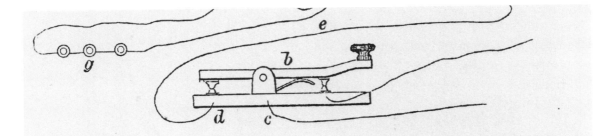

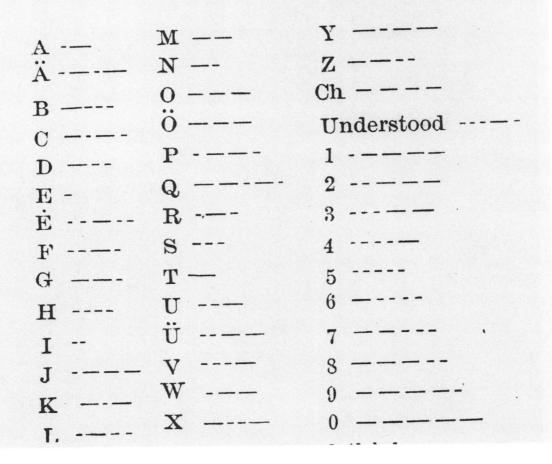

A ·—	M ——	Y —·——
Ä ·—·—	N —·	Z ——··
B —···	O ———	Ch ————
C —·—·	Ö ·——·	Understood ···—·
D —··	P ·——·	1 ·————
E ·	Q ——·—	2 ··———
Ė ··—··	R ·—·	3 ···——
F ·—··	S ···	4 ····—
G ——·	T —	5 ·····
H ····	U ··—	6 —····
I ··	Ü ··——	7 ——···
J ·———	V ···—	8 ———··
K —·—	W ·——	9 ————·
L ·—··	X —··—	0 —————

A Morse code alphabet sheet was used to translate the signals coming from telegraph operators.
Reproduced by permission of the Library of Congress.

On May 24, 1844, Morse sent a message from Baltimore, Maryland, to Washington D.C., a distance of about forty-five miles, over wires strung with the help of government financing. An associate in Washington sent the message back, confirming it had traveled round-trip in seconds. Suddenly, an invention that had been in development for over a decade became the talk of the town, in Washington and elsewhere. Newspaper writers were wildly enthusiastic about the possibilities for getting news, and conducting business, using the new technology.

For Morse, the moment of victory on that May day had been long in coming. He had been working on his invention for a decade, as had other engineers in Europe. In 1837 he had applied for a grant being offered by Congress to demonstrate a long-distance telegraph, but Congress did not get around to granting the money, $30,000, until near the end of 1843. The following May, Morse demonstrated his technology, which was almost immediately heralded in the press as a revolution in communications.

The telegraph sent electricity through wires to coil of wire, which caused metal in the center of the coil to become magnetized; the magnet, in turn, attracted metal, and enabled the receiver to record a series of long and short electrical signals. The principal contribution of Morse was developing a code, based on different combinations of long and short signals, that operators could translate into letters and numbers.

Morse kept a scrapbook of newspaper stories about the telegraph that is now in a collection at the Library of Congress in Washington, D.C. He did not always label the articles, so it is not always possible to determine what newspaper published them, or on what date. But these clippings, all from the 1840s, show how the country reacted to an invention that was similar to what the Internet is today. The telegraph may have been even more exciting when it was introduced, because no such means of communication had ever been seen before.

The telegraph became a vital component of the Industrial Revolution. With rapid communications, merchants could place, and fill, orders from far away in a more timely fashion. Factories could ship products to national markets instead of regional ones. Investors and businesses outside New York could be kept current on the price of stocks (shares of businesses) and other business and financial developments that affected them.

Reading newspaper articles published at the time the telegraph was brand new offers an insight into the excitement Morse's invention caused at the time.

Things to remember while reading newspaper accounts regarding the telegraph:

- Morse's first demonstration of his telegraph was in Washington, D.C.; later a message was sent over a wire from Washington to Baltimore, about forty-five miles away. The cost of stringing telegraph wires to connect the large cities of the United States was staggering, and Morse gave his demonstration to Congress as part of a campaign to gain support for government financing. Then, as now, there were arguments against using taxpayer dollars to finance an unproven technology, and many held the belief that the government had no business getting into an enterprise that could be funded by private investors (as many telegraph wires eventually were). On the other side were those who believed that the benefits of the telegraph to the whole nation were so great, the expense could be easily justified.

- It is not precisely correct to say that Morse invented the telegraph. Nearly a century before Morse's demonstration, in 1753, a writer known only as C. M. wrote an article in *Scots Magazine* describing a system to send messages using electricity sent over twenty-six wires, one for each letter of the alphabet. In 1837, two British inventors, William Cooke (1806–1879) and Charles Wheatstone (1802–1875), patented a successful telegraph system that sent messages a distance of about thirty miles, using five wires instead of one. In the United States, it was the combination of inventiveness and salesmanship that enabled Morse to get government money to finance his own system that used one wire and a unique code. Not only did Morse demonstrate the first practicable telegraph system over a long distance; he also was a tireless promoter of the telegraph as a superior means of communication.

- The style of newspaper writing in the 1840s was much different from what we are accustomed to today. Most newspapers were biased in favor of one or another political party and had no hesitation in denouncing politicians they did not care for. The telegraph changed the way that news was transmitted, and contributed to a more objective writing style, as papers of many different political persuasions were receiving the same stories via telegraph.

"The Age of Miracles"; clipping from the New York Herald, 1848

On the first of January, 1848, of the Christian era, the new age of miracles began—an age that will be more astonishing and wonderful than all the preceding ages of the world. We have had geological periods, traditionary eras, historical ages, and now we have just **commenced**, *on the 1st of January, 1848, the electric, or miraculous age, of the history of this world, and the races on it, that will far outstrip that of* **Moses and the Prophets**. *Printing was the first invention, steam was the next discovery, and the third was that of the electric telegraph. They are now combined in one movement, and have presented, during the last week, one of the first symptoms of the miraculous age, in the columns of the New York Herald....*

It is difficult, however, to convey to the public any idea of the wonderful combination by which these miracles are performed. Steam, electricity and machinery, operated upon by Heaven-born intellect, produce the whole. The result is, that space and time are **annihilated**. *By this wonderful process, the city of New York becomes the central point of the nation, and all the cities connected with it by telegraph, on the Atlantic sea board, become its faubourgs—its wards—communicating with them as rapidly and readily every hour, as Wall street does with Chambers street, or Astor Place does with the Park. In fact, time is not only beaten, but it is annihilated. We can send a message from New York to St. Louis at twelve o'clock at noon, and* it will reach its destination on the banks of the Mississippi at ten minutes before twelve....

The city of Washington, and Congress, are now part of the metropolis of New York, by means of the telegraph; and by our system of reporting and our machinery, we have accomplished the removal of the Capitol northward, even nearer than **Hoboken** *is to New York. These wonders of the week—these miracles of seven days—in the beginning of the year 1848, are only the first* **rude** *efforts of genius and art, directed to elements that will revolutionise the whole world in less than fifty years. Morse, the inventor of the telegraph,* **Hoe**, *the inventor of the new printing press, and those editors and conductors of public journals, who understand and have enterprise*

Commenced: Started.

Moses and the Prophets: A reference to figures in the Bible.

Annihilated: Wiped out.

Hoboken: A city in New Jersey across the Hudson River from New York City.

Rude: Basic.

Hoe: Richard M. Hoe (1812–1886), the inventor of a form of the printing press for use by newspapers.

to use those inventions and discoveries, and to combine them with intellect all together, will henceforth create a change in the history of the human race that will make them be remembered thousands of years hence, as the **Confuciuses**, or the **Mahomets**, or the **Zoroasters**, or the **Moseses** of the nineteenth century, in those matters which change the destiny of races, of nations, and of people....

The expense of this is great; but what of that? The American people love, adore, idolize, and cheerfully patronize and pay for enterprise, skill, **sagacity**, talent, genius, in the greatest and **sublimest**....

"Newspaper Enterprise—Extraordinary Express from Lexington, Kentucky"; clipping from the New York Herald, 1844

Probably one of the most remarkable feats of newspaper enterprise, is the result of that which appears in this morning's Herald—the speech and resolutions of **Mr. Clay**, delivered at Lexington [Kentucky] the day before yesterday.

The distance is nearly one thousand miles.—Knowing the importance of Mr. Clay's opinions and movements in the popular contest now about to take place in this country [the presidential election of 1844, in which Clay ran for president], we made extraordinary arrangements last week to run an Express exclusively for the Herald. We have, however, taken into the enterprise since our arrangements were made, two of our **cotemporaries**, who will also publish the same this morning.

About eleven or twelve o'clock, on the day before yesterday, the meeting was held at Lexington. Our reporters were there, and when the resolutions were read, and Mr. Clay had delivered his speech, our express started on horseback, running eighty-four miles, to Cincinnati. At Cincinnati the notes of our reporters were written out, and the whole was sent on through the electric telegraph, to this city, a distance of nearly a thousand miles. The speech and resolutions were received early yesterday morning, and, but for the intervention of Sunday, we should have been able to have published the whole Lexington proceedings in less than ten hours from their delivery in Kentucky.

This feat in newspaper enterprise has never yet been paralleled in the civilized world. In England, where journalism is carried on with more enterprise than in any other country, nothing has

Confuciuses: Those like Chinese philosopher Confucius (551–479 B.C.E.).

Mahomets: Those like Mohammed (570–632), prophet of Islam.

Zoroasters: Those like religious teacher Zoroaster (628–551 B.C.E.).

Moseses: Those like Moses (c. 1250 B.C.E.), prophet of Judaism.

Sagacity: Wisdom.

Sublimest: Most awe-inspiring.

Mr. Clay: Henry Clay (1777–1852), U.S. senator from Kentucky.

Cotemporaries: Alternate spelling of contemporaries; colleagues, co-workers.

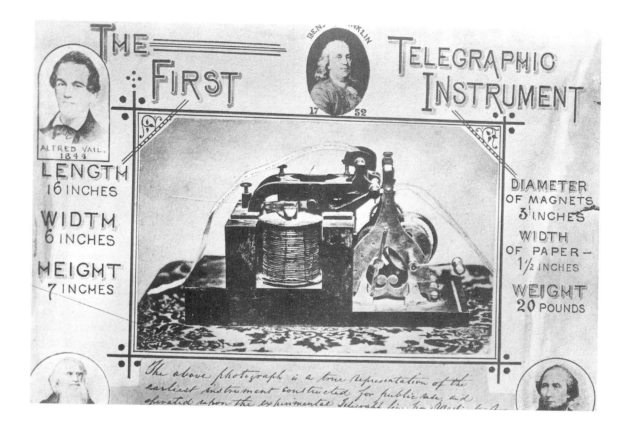

THE FIRST TELEGRAPHIC INSTRUMENT

ALFRED VAIL. 1844

BEN. FRANKLIN 1752

LENGTH
16 INCHES

WIDTH
6 INCHES

HEIGHT
7 INCHES

DIAMETER
OF MAGNETS
3 INCHES

WIDTH
OF PAPER —
1½ INCHES

WEIGHT
20 POUNDS

The above photograph is a true representation of the earliest instrument constructed for public use, and operated upon the experimental Telegraph line from Washington to

taken place which can be compared with this extraordinary fact. But this is not all. In less than six months, when the telegraphic wires shall be completed to New Orleans, and to other points, we expect to publish **intelligence** fifteen hundred or two thousand miles distant, the day after it transpires at all the different **extremities** of the **republic**.

Thus it will be seen, probably in the present year, that all this vast republic will be covered with telegraphic wires, and important intelligence from every extremity of the nation will be known every morning at New York, with as much accuracy and certainty as we know what has taken place in the City Hall. These wires may be extended to the Pacific, to California, to Oregon, and to every part of Mexico. It is no wonder, therefore, that the young spirit of the present age, the modern impulse of the American people, the great movement which is now urging on this mighty **Anglo-Saxon race**, paralyses, astonishes, transfixes, all the old politicians of the day, from Mr. Clay down to the lowest one that may hang upon the extremities of either party. Steam and electricity, with the natural im-

Alfred Vail (Samuel Morses's assistant) received the first telegraph message, sent from the United States Supreme Court Room to the Mount Clare railroad station in Baltimore, Maryland. *Reproduced by permission of Corbis.*

Intelligence: News.

Extremities: Far reaches.

Republic: The United States.

Anglo-Saxon race: People whose ancestors came from England or northern Europe.

*pulses of a free people, have made, and are making, this country the greatest, the most original, the most wonderful the sun ever shone upon. And if our great statesmen and our noisy Congress, do not comprehend the position in which they stand between the eternity of the past, and the eternity before them, they will be hurried out of the line of movement, and others will take their places. The **annexation** of Texas, the war with Mexico, the renovation of that country, are only part and parcel of the great and wonderful movement of the age, begun by the American people. Those who do not mix with this movement—those who do not become part of this movement—those who do not go on with this movement—will be crushed into more **impalpable** powder than ever was attributed to the car of **Juggernaut**. Down on your knees and pray.*

Newspaper clipping, title unknown, circa 1844

*Well, this Mr. Morse, during the last session of the **laborious, incorruptible**, and (of course?) much-abused Twenty-seventh Congress, made his appearance in the Capitol with an earnest request for the aid of Congress, to construct a telegraph on the plan of his new invention. The proposition was that this first line of electric wires, should be laid between Washington and Baltimore, and that Congress should **appropriate** $30,000 for its construction, it being impossible to obtain the necessary amount by individual contributions among the few who were intelligent enough to appreciate the value and feasibility of the enterprise.*

*To show to Members of Congress by actual experiment the principles and the mode of operation, Mr. Morse and **Mr. Vail** were hard at work at the two ends of the telegraphic wires for two or three months, sending messages back and forth to each other, as they were dictated by Members, for the sake of learning the character of the invention, and the reality of its wonderful **pretensions**. In the course of the session there was not a Member of either House, that had not an opportunity to become perfectly acquainted with it if he chose. This "Capitol affair" by the way, was probably the first Electric Telegraph ever put in operation for so great a distance.*

*Among the rest, **Millard Fillmore** was much interested with the novel and extraordinary machine, and in due time moved an amendment to the great annual civil appropriation bill, appropriating the required $30,000 for the construction of an electric telegraph from*

Annexation: Taking possession of.

Impalpable: Untouchable.

Juggernaut: Unstoppable force.

Laborious: Requiring a great deal of effort.

Incorruptible: Incapable of being morally corrupted.

Appropriate: To set aside for a particular use.

Mr. Vail: Alfred Vail, Samuel Morse's assistant.

Pretensions: Claims to fame.

Millard Fillmore (1800–1874): A future U.S. president, at the time a congressman from New York.

Washington to Baltimore, under the direction of Mr. Morse. Never was a motion so savagely, abusively, bitterly, **derisively** opposed, as this was by **Cave Johnson, Hop Turney**, and that sort of abominable **Locofocos**, who could not, and would not, be made to regard it as anything but a **humbug**, a worthless invention, a cheat. Cave Johnson raved and scolded, and ranted, and screamed, and foamed against the House, like a **demoniacally possessed** man. There never was an angrier man than he, when, under the urgent and impressive representations of Fillmore, the House, in spite of all these outrageous **clamors**, adopted the amendment. To give the hated telegraph one final expression of his baffled and stupid hostility, Cave Johnson then rose, and grinning with **impotent malice**, moved as a further amendment, an appropriation of sixty thousand dollars to carry on experiments in **Animal Magnetism**, as a doubly important and much more rational object!! This amendment was actually voted for by himself, and several Locofoco animals of the same breed, as an insult to Mr. Morse and Mr. Fillmore, and indeed the House itself!

Two years afterwards, this same ignorant, heartless blockhead [Cave Johnson] was made Postmaster-General, and put in charge of this same Telegraph, to direct its operations as the property of the government.

What happened next ...

By 1854, there were twenty-three thousand miles of telegraph wires being used in the United States, linking most of the major cities in the eastern half of the United States. In 1868 a telegraph cable was strung across the Atlantic, a distance of about five thousand miles.

The desire for faster, better communications continued well beyond the telegraph. In 1876 Alexander Graham Bell (1847–1922) demonstrated the first telephone used to transmit sound. A century later, in 1973, the U.S. Defense Department provided funding to develop a network linking computers, now called the Internet.

The telegraph also had profound effects on business. Tied together with rapid communication of news, the United

Derisively: Mockingly scornful.

Cave Johnson (1793–1866): U.S. Congressman from Texas opposed to Congress awarding Samuel Morse $30,000 in funding for experiments.

Hop Turnley (1797–1857): U.S. congressman and later senator from Tennessee.

Locofocos: Faction of the Democratic Party.

Humbug: Nonsense.

Demoniacally possessed: Taken over by the devil.

Clamors: Loud noises.

Impotent malice: Mean spiritedness.

Animal Magnetism: A discredited theory about electricity flowing through the body.

States became a single market for manufacturers. Investors were able to follow stock prices in New York, and it became possible to tap the savings of people all over the United States to raise the money (capital) needed to build large enterprises. New fortunes were made from instant knowledge of conditions (such as weather disasters) that affected the prices of crops. Without instant communications, pioneered by the telegraph, it is difficult to imagine the rapid growth of America's industrial economy.

Did you know ...

In 1848 six highly competitive newspapers in New York City agreed on a plan to share the expenses of sending news via telegraph. The newspapers formed an organization called the Associated Press (AP), which still serves the same purpose, long after telegraph wires have been superceded by high-speed electronic communications. Many newspapers belong to the AP and regularly print its stories from all over the United States and overseas. Newspapers also continue to contribute their own stories for use by the AP.

For more information

Books

Coe, Lewis. *The Telegraph: A History of Morse's Invention and Its Predecessors in the United States.* Jefferson, NC: McFarland, 1993.

Standage, Tom. *The Victorian Internet: The Remarkable Story of the Telegraph and the Nineteenth Century's On-line Pioneers.* New York: Walker and Co., 1998.

Periodicals

Totty, Michael. "Deja-vu: How the Internet Is Like, and Different from, Inventions of the Past." *Wall Street Journal*, July 15, 2002, p. R13.

Web Sites

"The Samuel F. B. Morse Papers at the Library of Congress, 1793–1919." *Library of Congress, American Memory Collections.* http://memory.loc.gov/ammem/sfbmhtml/sfbmhome.html (accessed on April 11, 2003).

J. D. B. Stillman

Excerpt from "The Last Tie"

Published in *Overland Monthly*, July 1869

The completion of a railroad linking the East Coast to the western United States, in Promontory, Utah, on May 10, 1869, was a famous event in the history of the expansion of the United States to include all of America. It was also an important symbol of how the Industrial Revolution—the process of incorporating machines and factories into manufacturing goods—was reshaping American society.

Dr. J. D. B. Stillman (1819–1888) of California recognized the importance of the new rail link in his eyewitness account of the ceremony that was held to mark the occasion, when a symbolic golden spike (nail) was pounded into the last tie, to hold that last rail in place and complete the railroad connection between the Atlantic and Pacific Oceans. ("Tie" has a double meaning here, as both a connection and the square timbers on which railroad tracks lie.)

Two months after the event, Stillman's article appeared in a San Francisco magazine, the *Overland Monthly*. In his article, Stillman recalled the first time he traveled from the East Coast to California, thirty years earlier. Then, it took a six-month ocean voyage around the tip of South America,

"Could I refuse to share in this triumph on the great day, long prayed for, that was to witness the finishing blow to the greatest enterprise of the age?"

The completion of the first transcontinental railroad at Promontory, Utah, in 1869, was a significant milestone in the Industrial Revolution and the advancement of the United States.
Reproduced by permission of the National Archives and Records Administration.

and Stillman recalled feeling that he had left the United States forever. Now, the eastern and western halves of the country were connected by a railroad, making possible a trip from San Francisco to New York in a few days, instead of the weeks or months that it previously required.

The completion of the transcontinental railroad was also a symbol of the advance of the Industrial Revolution. A journey that used to rely on animals (usually horses, to ride or to pull wagons), or on wind (to propel a sailing ship), was now possible using a mechanical device—a train pulled by a locomotive that used a steam engine.

The railroad link also meant that farmers in western states could send their crops to the populated East. This development was important for two reasons: first, it offered a market for farmers who were starting new farms in the American West; it also meant that farms in the West could produce food for the rapidly growing urban population of factory workers in the East.

The expansion of railroads into the West had another impact. By connecting farms with the eastern markets, the railroads encouraged people from Europe to immigrate to the United States and set up new farms. Businessman James J. Hill (1838–1916), who made a fortune building the Great Northern Railroad across the northern tier of states a few years later, understood this very clearly. He sent representatives to Europe, particularly to countries like Sweden and Norway, to encourage new immigrants. Hill, like other railroad owners, was given land in the West by the U.S. government in order to encourage building railroads. Hill and others could sell the land they were given to immigrants who wanted their own farms (and who also would provide crops for the railroad to haul back East).

J. D. B. Stillman. *Reproduced by permission of Getty Images.*

As part of the westward expansion of European settlement, new farm machines, such as the steel plow of John Deere (1837–1886) and the mechanical reaper of Cyrus McCormick (1809–1884), made farming large plots of land feasible. The expansion of railroads was a symbol of the rapid expansion of agriculture in the United States, which became one of the biggest food producers in the world at the same time it was becoming one of the biggest producers of manufactured goods.

Both the growth of large farms and the rise of urban factories marked a major change from the United States familiar to J. D. B. Stillman when he left the East for California.

What Time Is It?

The railroads contributed to another aspect of modern life that is closely associated with the Industrial Revolution—the idea of standard time.

Before about 1880, a jeweler who owned a clock set the local time by observing when the sun was directly overhead and setting his clock at noon. That clock would then be used to set the other clocks in town. As the Earth turns, the Sun appears to travel about twelve miles every minute. That means that in towns twelve miles apart (east to west), the moment of noon would be about a minute apart.

When travelers used horses or carriages, this time difference did not matter; in fact, it made sense, since noon was when the Sun was overhead. But for fast-moving trains, the difference of a minute every twelve miles was much more significant. Railroads need to keep on a schedule, especially since trains traveling in opposite directions often shared one pair of tracks. But if a train in one town said it was leaving at noon, what time would that be in a town that was, say, sixty-five miles to the west?

Part of the solution lay in the telegraph, which could send messages instantly over long distances, alerting one train that another was coming at it over the single set of rails. The telegraph also made it possible to agree on a standard moment for noon. A message could be sent to many towns instantly, stating that it was noon (regardless of exactly where the Sun was in the sky).

On November 18, 1883, the railroads agreed to set standard time in different time zones—Eastern, Central, Mountain, and Pacific—so that the minutes would be the same everywhere, and only the hours would change.

It was an idea that had been proposed as early as 1809, but it took the expansion of railroads across the continent to bring it into practice, although even then not every city went along. Detroit, Michigan, for example, did not finally adopt standard time until 1905, and then only after a prolonged debate.

His recollection of that earlier time summarizes the major change in society and industry over just three decades in the middle third of the nineteenth century.

Things to remember while reading the excerpt from "The Last Tie":

- The completion of the transcontinental railroad was well recognized as a major event at the time. Two companies, the Union Pacific laying track from the East to the West, and the Central Pacific, laying track from California to the East, had been in a fierce competition to see which company could lay tracks faster. Moreover, people at the time seemed to fully recognize the historic significance of the event, and the ceremony in Promontory, Utah, brought out the same sort of sightseers and souvenir hunters as might attend such an event today.

• In his opening paragraph, Stillman makes a pun on the word "tie." He thought his connection ("tie") to the East had been broken when he moved to California, but even then the wooden railroad tie that would become part of the transcontinental railroad was growing in the form of a tree that would later help reestablish old personal ties.

• At one point the author mentions that ten miles of track were laid in a single day, and he reckons that each man lifted 74 tons (148,000 pounds) of rail during that one day. His list of the workers who accomplished this includes mostly Irish names. Chinese workers also played a key role in constructing the western part of the line. When many European laborers rushed off to prospect (explore) for silver in Nevada, the railroad imported workers from China, whose efforts were critical in completing the line.

• The ceremony surrounding the pounding in of the last spike was elaborately arranged. According to other accounts of the moment, a spike of gold, representing the California gold rush, was carefully placed in a hole that had been predrilled (otherwise, the spike made of a soft metal like gold would have been crushed by a hammer). The governor of California, Leland Stanford (1824–1893; who was also president of the Pacific Central Railroad) picked up a mallet and took a mighty swing. He missed the spike and hit the wooden tie instead. Then a vice president of the Union Pacific, Thomas Durant (1820–1885), took a swing at a special silver spike contributed by Nevada (where silver had been discovered at the Comstock Lode in 1860). Suffering from a headache because he had attended a party the night before, Durant missed both the spike and the tie. Finally a regular railroad worker hammered in the spikes and a Western Union telegraph operator sent the signal to the waiting nation: "D-O-N-E."

• The author of this article uses several devices to present his story that cannot be taken literally. He did not have a dream, or reverie, even though he describes such a moment. The article is intended to review the significant progress over thirty years, a period during which the American frontier moved from just west of the Appalachian Mountains all the way to the Pacific Ocean. Stillman's article puts the two times next to each other to emphasize the speed and extent of change brought about, in large part, by the Industrial Revolution.

Excerpt from "The Last Tie"

*When we stood for the first time on the **iron-bound** shores of the Pacific a generation ago and looked upon their **desolate** mountains, after a voyage of more than half a year, we thought in our **forlorn** hearts that the last tie that bound us to our native land was broken. We did not dream that the tie that was to reunite us, and make this our native land forever, was then flourishing as a green bay tree in our woods; but even so it was, and here, in the month of May, it lay before us, a polished shaft, and in whose alternate veins of light and shade we saw symbolized the varied experience of our California life.*

*Would I accept an invitation to go to the "front" and see the last spike driven? Old veterans and companions in frontier life would be there—men with whom I had hunted grizzlies in the river jungles. We had hungered and feasted together on the Plains, slept with our feet to the same fire, and fevered side by side when the **miasma** had shrunk the blood of our veins. Could I refuse to share in this triumph on the great day, long prayed for, that was to witness the finishing blow to the greatest enterprise of the age? California would be there with her bridal gift of gold; Nevada and Arizona were coming with their silver **dowers**, and a telegram from Sacramento informed me that a place would be reserved for me in the special car that was to convey the high **contracting parties** of the first part to the scene of the memorable event....*

Across the bridge and out upon the plain we flew, alternate flashes of wheat fields and flowery pastures, and ghosts of trees

Iron-bound: Bordered by iron and other minerals.

Desolate: Uninhabited.

Forlorn: Lonely and sad.

Miasma: A vapor, such as tobacco smoke.

Dowers: Treasure, in this case, referring to silver spikes.

Contracting parties: Dignitaries.

went by; the rumble and clatter of car wheels filled my ears and soon lulled me into a drowsy *reverie*, and I "dreamed a dream that was not all a dream."

I stood as a child in my father's dooryard and saw the rippling flood as it flowed for the first time over the sandy floor of that stream—small as it seemed when measured by the line, but mighty in its results—that immortalized the name of **Clinton**, and opened the great lakes and prairies of the west to the commerce of the Atlantic. A troop of boys, barelegged, were frolicking in the frothy current; one stoops down and catches a fish struggling half smothered, and bears him away in exultation; the booming of cannon rolls their *paeans* of victory from the Hudson [River] to [Lake] Erie, and back again through a wilderness, startling the black bear from its *covert* and awakening the land of the **Iroquois** with the march of a mighty people.

Again I stood amidst a group of curious, skeptical men on "Albany Hill," when a ponderous steamer on wheels was about to test the practicability of making steam a motive power on railways. They

This campsite near the Humboldt River Canyon in Nevada was like many that housed workers building the transcontinental railroad. *Reproduced by permission of the National Archives and Records Administration.*

Reverie: Dream.

Clinton: DeWitt Clinton (1769–1828), governor of New York and supporter of the Erie Canal.

Paeans: Praises.

Covert: Hiding place.

Iroquois: Native American tribe.

had been successful in England, and why not here? A line of road had been constructed for fifteen miles as straight as a beam of light from the sun and at water level. I heard again the fizzing of the steam and the gush of water as the machine vainly **essayed** to start. More fuel was supplied, the fizzing grew louder and sharper—slowly the wheels began to revolve but slipped on the track—sand was thrown on, when, with a cheer from the hopeful, the enormous black mass began to move off. The crowd grew excited and followed on, men on horseback led the way, determined to be in at the death and see how far the joke would go. Faster the **iron horse** moved on, faster the horsemen rode, and as the dreadful sounds redoubled, their **steeds** bolted the course, with staring eyeballs, terror-stricken. The locomotive was the victor; one dog alone contested the race, bounding and barking on till lost in the distance, and on the long vista, where the paralleled lines met, the black speck disappeared, leaving a film of smoke to float away among the pines....

And still I dreamed; the air grew larger and darker, deeper and darker **yawned** the canyons, the train seemed poised in mid-air, now flying through tree-tops, and now circling like an eagle the **beetling** cliffs they call Cape Horn. Far below, rivers flowed like silken threads, and as silent; above us, the snowy peaks kept creeping down, and somber shadows of giant pines, whose vast trunks had withstood the storms for a thousand years, oppressed us with their gloom. We plunge into **the bowels of the mountains** and out at once into the sunlight and past the cheerful dwellings of men. We are cribbed in by timbers, snow-sheds they call them; but how strong! Every timber is a tree trunk, braced and bolted to withstand the snow-slide that starts in midwinter from the great heights above, and gathering volume as it descends, sweeps desolation in its path; the air is cold around us; snow is on every hand; it looks down upon us from the cliffs, up to us from the ravines, drips from overhead and is frozen into **stalactites** from the rocky wall along which our road is blasted, midway of [up] the granite mountain. We are in **pithy** darkness in the heart of the mountain—the summit of the grade; out again into the light; on, on through **wooden galleries** mile after mile; a **sylvan** lake flashes out from its emerald setting among the mountains—a well-dressed gentleman touches me on the arm, and taking a cigar from his lips, asks me if I will not take luncheon. "Where are we?" I responded. "There is Donner Lake and we will soon be at Truckee...."

At Elko [Nevada] we parted with the most of our passengers, who were bound for the White Pine country a hundred miles south

Essayed: Tried.

Iron horse: Locomotive.

Steeds: Horses.

Yawned: Opened wide.

Beetling: Jutting.

The bowels of the mountains: The depths of the mountains.

Stalactites: Needle-like accumulations of minerals found in caves.

Pithy: Related to the core.

Wooden galleries: Windows in the tunnel.

Sylvan: Forest.

of the railroad. Another night brought us to the front, where we saw the novel sight of a town on wheels. Houses built on cars to be moved as the work progressed. Here were the **Chinamen** who had built more railroad in a given time than was ever done before by any people. The Central Pacific Company had been battling for years with the **formidable** difficulties of the **Sierra Nevadas**; and when at length they descended from the mountains they passed like a hurricane across the open country. All the material except the lumber was transported around the continent; and yet with such **vigor** was the work pushed forward, that three hundred miles of the road was constructed in nine months. Ten miles of track were laid in one day; and it is worthy of note, that all the rails were taken from the trucks and deposited in their places by eight men, four on a side. These rails weigh on an average five hundred and sixty pounds; and allowing fifty feet to each rail, the amount of iron **borne** by each man during the day of eleven hours was seventy-four tons! This was **without relay**. The names of the men who performed this feat are justly a part of this record. They were: Michael Shay, Patrick Joyce, Thomas Dailey, Michael Kennedy, Frederick McNamara, Edward Killeen, Michael Sullivan, and George Wyatt.

We arrived at Promontory Summit on Friday, under the information that the connection of the two roads would be made on the following day. The morning was rainy and dreary; two or three tents were pitched in the vicinity for the **rendezvous** of those **ruffians** who hang about on the march of industry, and flourish on the vices of men. The telegraph operators at the end of the respective lines were then within a few rods of each other, and communication was open with the **officers** of the Union line to the eastward of us. We were informed, after some delay, that it would be impossible for them to arrive before Monday [that is, they would be late for the ceremony]. The delay seems to have been an unavoidable one; but it was to cause a great disappointment to the people of California, whose arrangements for a celebration the next day were completed. The intelligence was sent back to Sacramento and San Francisco; and messages were returned that the celebration must take place according to the published programme; that it could not be delayed without defeating its object altogether. We all felt the embarrassment of our position keenly; but we tried to make the best of circumstances we could not control. To spend three days in this desolate spot, surrounded with sage-brush, with only such neighbors as would make it dangerous to venture away from the car, lest we have our throats cut the suspicion that we might have a spare quar-

Chinamen: Term commonly used during this era to describe those of Chinese descent.

Formidable: Causing fear or dread.

Sierra Nevadas: Range of mountains.

Vigor: Energy.

Borne: Carried.

Without relay: Without a break.

Rendezvous: Meeting.

Ruffians: Gangs.

Officers: Executives.

ter in our pockets, was not charming. The camps of the construction parties of each road had fallen back from the summit to the low ground near the lake, after the close of one of the most celebrated contests of engineering skill and energy on both sides ever known, and were resting on their arms.

One-half of our party **procured** a **conveyance** to the camps of the Union Pacific, where General Casement, their Superintendent of Construction, generously dispatched a train to convey them to Ogden [Utah]. On the following day the same **gallant** officer came up to the end of his track, with a special train which he put at the disposal of Governor Stanford to take the rest of us over their road. The offer was accepted, and we ran down to Weber Creek station, and an opportunity was enjoyed of viewing some of the finest mountain scenery in the world. The Wasatch Mountains rise from the plain on the west shore of the lake to the height of six thousand feet above its surface, or ten thousand feet above the level of the sea. They are very ideal of inaccessible snow-covered mountains, set off by the green fields and blushing tints of the peach orchards just coming into flower. Mr. Hart, the Central Pacific artist, who accompanied us, took some fine views of this mountain from the railway over-looking the town of Ogden. The **tiderip** is well marked where the currents of traffic from East and West greets the corn from Illinois, where paper is currency, and coal takes the place of Juniper trees as fuel. We feel, while looking about, that we have met half way. A genuine thunder storm seemed to have been got up for the occasion and drove us all indoors, while we were at Ogden, and cooled the air. Here we found plants common at the East, but unknown in California—as the old familiar Taraxicum or Dandelion; and Rhus toxicodendron or Poison Ivy takes the place of the Rhus diversiloba or Poison Oak....

On the morning of the tenth, as we looked out of the car, we saw a force of Union Pacific men at work closing up the gap that had been left at their end of the road, and the construction trains brought up large numbers of men to witness the laying of the last rail. About ten o'clock the whistle announced the long-expected officers from the other side. We went over at once to meet them. In a superb piece of cabinetwork, they call a **"Pullman car,"** we met **Vice President Durant**, of whom we have heard so much, with a black velvet coat and gay neck-tie, that seemed to have been the "last tie" to which he had been giving his mind, gorgeously gotten up. **General Dodge** was there, and he looked all business.... General Dodge on the part of the Union Pacific, and

Procured: Acquired.

Conveyance: Transportation.

Gallant: Brave.

Tiderip: Location.

Pullman car: A railroad passenger car with elaborate furnishings.

Vice President Durant: Thomas Durant (1820–1885), vice president of the Union Pacific Railroad.

General Dodge: General Greenville Dodge (1831-1916), construction supervisor of the Union Pacific portion of the railroad.

Edgar Mills on the part of the Central Pacific, were appointed to arrange the preliminaries.

The **munificence** of private citizens of San Francisco had contributed two gold spikes, each designed to be the last one driven. Gentlemen from Nevada had contributed a silver one, at whose forging a hundred men had each struck a blow. The Governor of Arizona, also on behalf of his Territory, had one of silver. The **Laurel** tie that we brought with us was adjusted to its place; and in order that each gold spike should be the last, one was presented by **Governor Stanford,** President of the Central Pacific, to Vice President Durant, of the Union Pacific, who should drive it as the last on the latter road, while the other was to be the last on the Central road, and be driven last of all by Governor Stanford, who had thrown the first shovelful of earth at the opening of the road.

It had been arranged with Mr. Gamble, superintendent of the telegraph lines, that throughout the cities of the United States, wherever fire-alarm telegraphs were established, connection should be made with the last spike and the hammer that drove it, so that the blow should announce itself and fire cannon on the shores of both oceans at the same instant. Preparations having completed, the operator sent notice to all stations throughout the country to be ready, and the whole nation held its breath. A reverend gentleman present was invited to invoke the blessing of Almighty God upon the work. The operator announced: "Hats off, prayer is being said;" and as we uncovered our heads, the crowds that were gathered at the various telegraph offices in the land uncovered theirs. It was a **sublime** moment, and we realized it. The prayer ended, the silver spikes were driven. Durant drove his of gold. Stanford stood with the silver sledge gleaming in the air, whose blow was to be heard farther, without metaphor, than any blow struck by mortal man; the realization of the ancient myth of Jupiter with the thunderbolt in his hand. The blow fell, and simultaneously the roar of cannon on both shores of the continent announced the tidings: It is done! The alarm bells of the principal cities struck, one—two—three—**synchronous** with the strokes of the hammer; and people rushed from their houses, thinking a general alarm of fire was being rung. The cause soon became known, and banners everywhere were flung to the breeze; other bells joined in the cry of joy and of triumph. **Te Deum Laudamus** was sung in the churches, and the chimes rung out the national anthems. The nation made a day of it....

Edgar Mills: Sacramento, California, businessman who was master of ceremonies for the event.

Munificence: Generosity.

Laurel: A type of evergreen tree.

Governor Stanford: Leland Stanford (1824–1893), governor of California, railroad builder.

Sublime: Awe-inspiring.

Synchronous: Happening at the same time.

Te Deum Laudamus: A church hymn whose Latin title means "We Praise Thee, O God."

*The prearranged telegrams to the President of the United States, the Associated Press, and others, were sent off; and after cheering the companies and everybody interested, we **adjourned** to the car of Mr. Durant, when answers to our messages began to pour in from Chicago, New York, and Washington, announcing that the lines worked as intended, and that the country was in ablaze everywhere at the East....*

*Years to come, the traveler as he passes the place will look out for the laurel tie and the gold and silver spikes that garnished the last rail that connected the two oceans with a continuous band of iron. Could they hope to see them there? Why, even before the officials left the spot they were removed and their places supplied with those of the ordinary material, and when the **throng** rushed up, the **coveted** prize was not there. What their fate would have been we can judge by that of their successors, which had to be replaced by new ones even before we left the spot. They were broken to pieces for **relics**; and the unfortunate rail itself was failing beneath the blows of hammers and stones, to be borne away in fragments as **heirlooms**.*

What happened next ...

The completion of the rail line linking the Atlantic and Pacific coasts of the United States was just the start of many railroads that rapidly covered the United States in the last half of the nineteenth century. The expansion of the railroads was a key factor in the Industrial Revolution for several reasons:

- The railroads were the largest single customer for the newly developed steel industry, as steel proved more suitable for rails than iron.

- Railroads were a critical factor in creating monopolies (exclusive control by one company) in some industries. Railroads granted special discounts to some producers of coal and steel, for example, allowing them to offer their goods at reduced prices and drive their competitors out of business.

- The monopolies in turn created a public outcry and led directly to government intervention in the "free market," such as the 1890 Sherman Antitrust Act, which gave the federal government the right to regulate corporations.

Did you know ...

On April 28, 1869, work crews of the Central Pacific Railroad laid ten miles of track in a single day. It is a record that in 2002 remained unbroken.

For more information

Books

Ambrose, Stephen E. *Nothing Like It in the World: The Men Who Built the Transcontinental Railroad, 1863–1869.* New York: Simon and Schuster, 2000.

Bain, David Haward. *Empire Express: Building the First Transcontinental Railroad.* New York: Viking, 1999.

Hogg, Garry. *Union Pacific: The Building of the First Transcontinental Railroad.* New York: Walker, 1969.

Stein, R. C. *The Transcontinental Railroad in American History.* Springfield, NJ: Enslow Publishers, 1997.

Stillman, J. D. B. "The Last Tie." *Overland Monthly,* July 1869.

Web Sites

"The Last Spike." *National Park Service.* http://www.nps.gov/gosp/history/spike.html (accessed on April 11, 2003).

Working Conditions

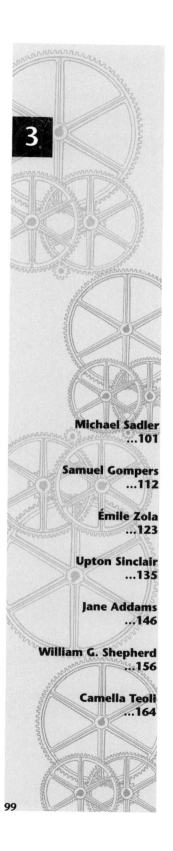

The new machines developed during the Industrial Revolution, beginning in the middle of the eighteenth century, used steam engines or running water (rivers and streams) to provide power. To house such machines, factories were built.

For most of the nineteenth century and into the twentieth, these factories, as well as the coal mines that supplied fuel for the steam engines, were the scenes of some of the most horrific working conditions ever known. In the absence of laws regulating the maximum work day or the minimum age of employment, men, women, and children toiled for twelve hours a day with barely a break. Conditions inside factories were often filthy and hazardous, and workers were often in danger of being maimed or killed as a result of industrial accidents.

These conditions came to the attention of journalists, novelists, and politicians who were horrified by what they saw and tried to bring about change by writing books, magazine and newspaper articles, or holding official hearings during which abused workers, especially children, told about their everyday lives. The public was exposed to the conditions of laborers and change was demanded.

Michael Sadler (1780–1835), a member of the British Parliament, issued the Sadler Report, bringing to light the findings of his investigation into child labor in factories. Émile Zola (1840–1908) wrote a novel depicting the conditions for workers in the coal mines of northern France.

In the United States, Congress held public hearings to investigate child labor, and workers like Camella Teoli were called to describe their experiences to lawmakers. Novelist Upton Sinclair (1878–1968) described the atmosphere for laborers in the Chicago stockyards in his landmark work *The Jungle.* Sometimes poor working conditions resulted in tragedy, such as the devastating fire at the Triangle Shirtwaist Company, which journalist William G. Shepherd chronicled for newspaper readers. America's first social worker, Jane Addams (1860–1935), also contributed to the written record of the impact of the Industrial Revolution in her autobiography *Twenty Years at Hull-House.*

In other cases, workers took the initiative to improve their own situation by organizing labor unions, groups that then bargained with employers for higher pay or improved working conditions. Samuel Gompers (1850–1924) was a leading organizer of unions, starting with a union of cigar makers and eventually leading the American Federation of Labor (AFL), which represented highly skilled workers. Gompers was inially motivated by the cramped, dark, and smelly houses where cigar makers both worked and lived in New York City.

Michael Sadler

Excerpt from the Sadler Report

**Transcripts of hearings held in 1831 and 1832
published in Paliamentary Papers in 1833**

In January 1833 the British Parliament published transcripts of hearings conducted by one of its members, Michael Sadler (1780–1835), a year earlier. Sadler was a well-known author of pamphlets urging better treatment of factory workers, and in 1832 he conducted a parliamentary investigation into the condition of children working in textile mills. As chairman of a parliamentary committee, Sadler had interviewed eighty-nine child workers in an effort to persuade the British Parliament to enact new laws to safeguard the rights of child workers. In Britain at the time, children just eight or nine years old regularly worked for twelve hours a day in textile mills.

The Sadler Report, as the hearings were called, had a major impact at the time of publication and for many decades later. Although Sadler had lost his seat in Parliament in the election of 1832, his report was published and provoked a public outcry against the practice of requiring young children to work for eleven or twelve hours a day. It led to new laws that restricted how many hours young children could work (but did not outlaw the practice of employing children in the first place).

The British Parliament building in London. Member of Parliament Michael Sadler conducted hearings regarding his investigation into the conditions of children working in textile mills. *Reproduced by permission of Susan D. Rock.*

Even into the twentieth century, the Sadler Report was often cited as evidence of how the Industrial Revolution (the process of introducing new machines and factories into the manufacturing of products) caused suffering for workers. The evidence given in the Sadler Report has been offered as a reason for close government regulation of factory owners. On the other hand, some critics accused Sadler of distorting the picture of conditions in English mills, making the situation appear worse than it was by selecting only the most outrageous cases to publicize.

Employing children in factories was not new in 1832; the practice had gone on for years as the Industrial Revolution transformed the textile (the practice of making yarn from cotton or wool and weaving it into fabric) industry, starting in the last quarter of the 1700s. New machines had been introduced that had resulted in spinning and weaving being moved out of family businesses, usually situated in homes, into huge factories. More than any other single industry, textiles represented the changes brought about by the Industrial Revolution.

Things to remember while reading the excerpt from the Sadler Report:

- Although the Sadler Report made a big impact on the British public when it was published in early 1833, it had severe critics. Some accused Sadler of phrasing the questions he asked young workers in a certain way to elicit responses that would support his campaign for new regulations by putting factories in a bad light. These critics asserted that the report was slanted from the beginning against mill owners, and that the outcome was predetermined. On the other hand, in the twenty-first century the Sadler Report is considered the classic description of the abuse of child laborers during the 1800s.

- For many children, the money they earned was critical to help their families make a living. But as employment of children became more controversial, many mill owners decided not to hire young employees, rather than have to worry about government inspectors and negative publicity. The result was that families lost the income from child workers, and suffered for it.

Excerpt from the Sadler Report

Testimony of Peter Smart

You say you were locked up night and day?

Yes.

Do the children ever attempt to run away?

Very often.

Were they pursued and brought back again?

Yes, the overseer pursued them, and brought them back.

Did you ever attempt to run away?

Yes, I ran away twice.

And you were brought back?

Yes; and I was sent up to the master's loft, and thrashed with a whip for running away.

*Were you **bound** to this man?*

Yes, for six years.

By whom were you bound?

My mother got 15 shillings [a unit of British currency] for the six years.

Do you know whether the children were, in point of fact, compelled to [work] during the whole time for which they were engaged?

Yes, they were.

Bound: Required to work under contract.

By law?

*I cannot say by law; but they were compelled by the **master**; I never saw any law used there but the law of their own hands.*

To what mill did you next go?

To Mr. Webster's, at Battus Den, within eleven miles of Dundee.

In what situation did you act there?

*I acted as **overseer**.*

At 17 years of age?

Yes.

Did you inflict the same punishment that you yourself had experienced?

I went as an overseer; not as a slave, but as a slave-driver.

What were the hours of labour in that mill?

*My master told me that I had to produce a certain quantity of yarn; the hours were at that time fourteen; I said that I was not able to produce the quantity of yarn that was required; I told him if he took the **timepiece** out of the mill I would produce that quantity, and after that time I found no difficulty in producing the quantity.*

How long have you worked per day in order to produce the quantity your master required?

*I have **wrought** nineteen hours.*

*Was this a **water-mill**?*

Yes, water and steam both.

To what time have you worked?

I have seen the mill going till it was past 12 o'clock on the Saturday night.

*So that the mill was still working on the **Sabbath** morning?*

Yes.

Were the workmen paid by the piece, or by the day?

No, all had stated wages.

*Did not that almost compel you to use great severity to the **hands** then under you?*

*Yes; I was compelled often to beat them, in order to get them to attend to their work, from their being **over-wrought**.*

*Were not the children exceedingly **fatigued** at that time?*

Master: Owner.

Overseer: Manager.

Timepiece: Clock.

Wrought: Worked.

Water-mill: Mill in which a waterwheel in a steam or river powered the equipment

Sabbath: Sunday; a day of worship.

Hands: Employees.

Over-wrought: Overworked.

Fatigued: Tired.

FACTS AND FICTION BY THE BEST OF THE

THE·MASSES

A·MONTHLY·MAGAZINE
DEVOTED·TO·THE·INTERESTS
OF·THE·WORKING·PEOPLE

MAY,
1912

PR
10 CE

Drawn for The Masses by Alice Beach Winter.

"WHY MUST I WORK?"

CONCERNING CHRISTIAN CHARITY - - By WILL IRV
THE DAY OF A MAN - - - By MARY HEATON VO

Yes, exceedingly fatigued.

Were the children bound in the same way in that mill?

No; they were bound from one year's end to another, for twelve months.

Did you keep the hands locked up in the same way in that mill?

*Yes, we locked up the mill; but we did not lock the **bothy**.*

Bothy: Booth; part of a factory.

Who Was Michael Sadler?

Michael Sadler (1780–1835) was a British member of Parliament when he held hearings, in 1832, into the working conditions of children employed in British textile factories. The stories the children told helped lead to new laws regulating the conditions under which children could be employed.

Sadler was born in Snelston, England, in 1780. When he was twenty, he moved to the growing town of Leeds, England, a center of the textile industry. There, he, his brother, and his father established a company to import linen from Ireland. Sadler became concerned about the issue of children employed on farms and in factories.

He published a number of pamphlets on the subject, starting with *The State and Prospects of the Country* (1829). Others included *The Factory Girl's Last Day* (1830), *On Poor Laws for Ireland* (1830), *On Ministerial Plan of Reform* (1831), and *On the Distress of the Agricultural Labourers* (1831).

In 1829 Sadler was elected to Parliament. Two years later he launched a campaign to improve working conditions for farmworkers, including providing better housing by churches (which were supported by taxpayers in England) and granting workers plots of land for gardens and raising cows for milk.

In March 1832 Sadler proposed laws to improve the lives of children working in British textile factories, including limiting the workday to ten hours. At first he had little support, but in April he began three months of public hearings during which eighty-nine child factory workers were interviewed, bringing to light the horrific conditions endured by young children.

Sadler lost his seat in Parliament at the next general election, also in 1832. But his report on child labor was still published, in January 1833. Its contents shocked the British public, and Sadler's campaign found new champions in Parliament. His report also became a classic source of information about the nature of the Industrial Revolution in the early nineteenth century.

Sadler died two and a half years later, in July 1835, in Belfast, Ireland.

Did you find that the children were unable to pursue their labour properly to that extent?

Yes; they have been brought to that condition, that I have gone and fetched up the doctor to them, to see what was the matter with them, and to know whether they were able to rise or not able to rise; they were not at all able to rise; we have had great difficulty in getting them up.

When that was the case, how long have they been in bed, generally speaking?

Perhaps not above four or five hours in their beds.

Testimony of Elizabeth Bentley

What age are you?

Twenty-three.

Where do you live?

At Leeds.

What time did you begin to work at a factory?

When I was six years old.

At whose factory did you work?

Mr. Busk's.

What kind of mill is it?

Flax-mill.

What was your business in that mill?

*I was a little **doffer**.*

What were your hours of labour in that mill?

*From 5 in the morning till 9 at night, when they were **thronged**.*

For how long a time together have you worked that excessive length of time?

For about half a year.

What were your usual hours when you were not so thronged?

From 6 in the morning till 7 at night.

What time was allowed for your meals?

Forty minutes at noon.

Had you any time to get your breakfast or drinking?

No, we got it as we could.

And when your work was bad, you had hardly any time to eat it at all?

No; we were obliged to leave it or take it home, and when we did not take it, the overlooker took it, and gave it to his pigs.

Flax-mill: Place that processed flax, or fiber, for yarn and linen.

Doffer: A worker who replaced bobbins, spools onto which newly spun yarn was wound, with empty spools.

Thronged: Very busy.

Do you consider doffing a laborious employment?

Yes.

Explain what it is you had to do?

*When the **frames** are full, they have to stop the frames, and take the **flyers** off, and take the full **bobbins** off, and carry them to the **roller**; and then put empty ones on, and set the frame going again.*

Does that keep you constantly on your feet?

Yes, there are so many frames, and they run so quick.

Your labour is very excessive?

Yes; you have not time for any thing.

*Suppose you **flagged** a little, or were too late, what would they do?*

***Strap** us.*

Are they in the habit of strapping those who are last in doffing?

Yes.

Constantly?

Yes.

Girls as well as boys?

Yes.

Have you ever been strapped?

Yes.

Severely?

Yes.

Could you eat your food well in that factory?

No, indeed I had not much to eat, and the little I had I could not eat it, my appetite was so poor, and being covered with dust; and it was no use to take it home, I could not eat it, and the over-looker took it, and gave it to the pigs.

You are speaking of the breakfast?

Yes.

How far had you to go for dinner?

We could not go home to dinner.

Where did you dine?

In the mill.

Frames: Spinning machines.

Flyers: Parts of a textile spinning machine.

Bobbins: Spools onto which newly spun yarn was wound.

Roller: Part of a textile spinning machine.

Flagged: Worked more slowly.

Strap: Punish; hit with a belt.

Did you live far from the mill?

Yes, two miles.

Had you a clock?

No, we had not.

Supposing you had not been in time enough in the morning at these mills, what would have been the consequence?

*We should have been **quartered**.*

What do you mean by that?

If we were a quarter of an hour too late, they would take off half an hour; we only got a penny an hour, and they would take a halfpenny more.

The fine was much more considerable than the loss of time?

Yes.

Were you also beaten for being too late?

No, I was never beaten myself, I have seen the boys beaten for being too late.

Were you generally there in time?

*Yes; my mother had been up at 4 o'clock in the morning, and at 2 o'clock in the morning; the **colliers** used to go to their work about 3 or 4 o'clock, and when she heard them stirring she has got up out of her warm bed, and gone out and asked them the time; and I have sometimes been at Hunslet Car at 2 o'clock in the morning, when it was streaming down with rain, and we have had to stay until the mill was opened.*

Quartered: Docked in pay.

Colliers: Coal miners.

What happened next ...

In July 1832 Sadler learned that at least half a dozen of the children interviewed had been fired for talking about the conditions in the factories where they had worked. He decided not to interview any more child workers, but instead to interview doctors who treated people working in textile factories, as a means of indirectly getting information about the plight of workers.

Later in the year, a meeting was held at York, England, at which sixteen thousand people gathered to express appreciation to Michael Sadler for shedding light on the conditions of work in textile mills. But the voters (limited to property owners and usually not including workers) did not appreciate his efforts. In a general election in 1832, Sadler was defeated by John Marshall, a major factory owner. Sadler had lost his seat in Parliament and with it the ability to bring the national spotlight on abuses of the factory system.

However, another British politician, Anthony Ashley Cooper (also known as Lord Ashley; 1801–1885), took up the cause of factory reform. The 1833 Factory Act, passed under Lord Ashley's leadership, made it illegal to employ children under age nine, and set a maximum eight-hour day for children between ages nine and thirteen.

Did you know ...

Friedrich Engels, coauthor of *The Communist Manifesto* (see entry), was hardly a friend of factory owners. But he did not think much of the Sadler Report. In his own book, *The Condition of the Working Class in England* (1844), Engels denounced Sadler's report this way:

> Sadler was led astray by his passionate sympathies into making assertions of a most misleading and erroneous [false] kind. He asked witnesses questions in such a way as to elicit answers which, although correct, nevertheless were stated in such a form as to give a wholly false impression.

For more information

Books

Engels, Friedrich. *The Condition of the Working Class in England*. 1844. Reprint, New York: Oxford University Press, 1993.

Hobbs, Sandy, Jim McKechnie, and Michael Lavalette. *Child Labor: A World History Companion*. Santa Barbara, CA: ABC-CLIO, 1999.

Ranta, Judith A. *Women and Children of the Mill: An Annotated Guide to Nineteenth-Century American Textile Factory Literature*. Westport, CT: Greenwood Press, 1999.

Ward, J. T. *The Factory Movement, 1830–1855*. New York: St. Martin's Press, 1962.

Williams, Mary E., ed. *Child Labor and Sweatshops*. San Diego, CA: Greenhaven Press, 1999.

Web Sites

Del Col, Laura. "The Life of the Industrial Worker in Nineteenth-Century England" (includes excerpt from the Sadler Report). *The Victorian Web*. http://www.cyberartsweb.org/victorian/history/workers1.html#sadler (accessed on April 10, 2003).

Samuel Gompers

Excerpt from "Tenement-House Cigar Manufacture"

Published in the *New Yorker Volkszeitung*, October 31, 1881

"For many years the system of tenement-house cigar manufacture has formed one of the most dreadful, cancerous sores in our city."

Samuel Gompers (1850–1924) is best known as the leader of the American Federation of Labor, a group of unions (organizations of workers) representing workers with special skills, such as weavers or carpenters. Before he came to national prominence as a leader of the labor movement, he was active in organizing a union of cigar makers.

In 1881, when Gompers was thirty-one years old, he wrote a series of articles in a German-language newspaper in New York City, the *New Yorker Volkszeitung* (New York Peoples' Newspaper), describing the living and working conditions of people who worked in cigar factories located in tenement houses. Tenement houses were narrow, run-down apartment houses built right next to one another; the houses Gompers describes were located in a neighborhood of Manhattan (in New York City) called the Lower East Side. Because they only had windows on two sides, the front and back, they were often dark and lacked good ventilation.

In these buildings, cigar makers worked in spaces that doubled as living quarters. As described by Samuel

Gompers, a typical family lived in three rooms: a bedroom, a room where cigars were made, and a kitchen. Usually the entire family was engaged in the process of making cigars. Because they were paid by the cigar, life was reduced to rolling cigars for twelve hours—or more—a day, then sleeping, and waking in order to make more cigars. Merchants delivered tobacco leaves to the cramped quarters; the leaves gave off an overpowering smell that lingered in the poorly ventilated rooms.

Gompers was inspired to write his own articles by a series of newspaper articles in the *New York Times* that had run ten years earlier, exposing corruption in city government. As he notes in the introduction to his articles, no one did anything about the corruption until the *New York Times* provided exact details about the wrongdoing. It was Gompers's aim to provide such details about tenement house factories in order to arouse public disgust and bring about government action.

Samuel Gompers (center) with leaders of the American Federation of Labor in 1916. Gompers exposed the working conditions in cigar factories located in tenement buildings in New York City. *Reproduced by permission of the Library of Congress.*

Things to remember while reading the excerpt from "Tenement-House Cigar Manufacture":

- Samuel Gompers was a cigar maker and understood the business from the inside. The use of children as workers from a very young age was a practice not limited to cigar-making in the 1880s. Child labor and substandard living conditions were common in many other industries. As the nineteenth century progressed, articles like Gompers's succeeded in creating a public uproar and resulted in legislation to ban child labor.

- Gompers believed that he needed to paint a vivid word picture of cigar makers' conditions in order to be effective. Rather than simply saying that workers lived in poor conditions, he went to the trouble of measuring the rooms, even the size of the windows, in order to give readers a precise picture of the harsh conditions in which cigar-makers and their families lived.

- In order to put the wages and rents mentioned by Gompers into context, the dollar amounts have been translated into current values. One dollar in 1881 would be worth about $18.17 in 2003, according to the Federal Reserve Bank of Minneapolis. In the text below, the dollar values in 2003 are in brackets after the amounts mentioned in the original text. For example: $7 [$127] means that a rent of $7 in 1881 would be equivalent to a rent of $127 in 2003.

Excerpt from "Tenement-House Cigar Manufacture"

*For many years the system of **tenement-house** cigar manufacture has formed one of the most dreadful, cancerous sores in our city: In every way, whether in regard to the wage conditions of the workers and not only that of the tenement-house workers—or their existence as human beings or family members, or the influence it has upon the immediate surroundings of the tenement factories and indirectly upon all the working population of the city, every year this system proves itself more of a **veritable plague** spot in the already*

Tenement-house: Cramped apartment building.

Veritable plague: Virtual disaster.

quite corrupt economic and social life of New York. The truth of this assertion has been recognized often enough in so-called "decisive" places, and most recently **Mayor Grace** expressed his intention of attacking this **pernicious** institution.

Unfortunately, the impressions produced in people by general assertions of grievances, no matter how well-grounded they may be, are usually not very deep or lasting. Only when precise and authentic details allow the public to gain insight into the actual character of the evils we **reproach** are people set into motion and one can count on finding the appropriate support for an **agitation** to abolish the grievances. One of the most striking examples of all times of this tendency is the fall of the **Tweed Ring**. Long before its collapse there was scarcely anyone in the city of New York who was not convinced that Tweed and his companions were daily and hourly **plundering** the city in the most shameful way. Despite all this, no movement to oust the scoundrels could be launched successfully. Only when the **"Times"** produced that famous **expose** which gave very precise details about the specific fraudulent transactions of city officials did a storm of **indignation** arise in the public which then swept the whole gang of political crooks out of public life.

Proceeding from this standpoint we have made it our business, through an exact examination of the facts and through publication of the results obtained … to provide the necessary factual foundation for those oft-repeated general assertions about the dreadful conditions produced by the tenement-factory system. This is no longer a matter of phrases but of facts and figures that cannot be argued away and that are well suited to horrify the reader who has had no previous idea of the depth of this **abyss**.

We hope the results of these publications will provide a lever that will at least contribute to preparing as quick an end as possible to that institution which is a burning humiliation to the so highly praised culture of our day and of our country.

In presenting to the readers of the N.Y. Volkszeitung the results of a careful examination of tenement-house cigar manufacture, of its system, the circumstances under which it takes place, and the dreadful consequences that inevitably result from it, we ask that attention be paid to the fact that the information depends in part on the degree of willingness of those most immediately involved, that is, the workers themselves, to inform us about their conditions. Since these workers are in constant fear not only of losing their jobs but also of being **evicted** from their apartments, it is natural for them to

Mayor Grace: William Grace (1832–1904), mayor of New York.

Pernicious: Destructive.

Reproach: Punish.

Agitation: Attempt to arouse public feeling.

Tweed Ring: Political organization in New York City that aligned itself with Democratic Party officeholders to steal public money; run by William Marcy Tweed (1823–1878).

Plundering: Stealing from.

Times: *The New York Times,* a newspaper.

Expose: A formal statement of facts.

Indignation: Anger aroused by something unjust.

Abyss: Intellectual or moral depth.

Evicted: Removed.

Crowded tenement
buildings housed cigar
factories and their families
in squalid conditions.
*Reproduced by permission of
the Library of Congress.*

regard with suspicion every stranger who attempts to gain precise information about their situation. Although it is fairly safe to assume that everything which the reporter learned about the conditions of the workers, not through his own observations but through what the workers told him themselves, still makes the situation appear far more favorable than it really is, there were nevertheless no attempts made in the following reports to express **speculations** or assumptions that would alter the actual facts. On the contrary, the following remarks, without any coloration or exaggeration, are a true mirror of that which our thoroughly objective reporter saw and heard. Since we will refrain from making the required commentary on the results of the investigation, without further introduction we begin with the presentation of our reporter which in its almost photographic way speaks an eloquent and terrible language.

HERMANN BLASKOPF'S TENEMENT-HOUSE FACTORY

No. 90 Cannon St. [in New York City], was the first of these buildings visited by this writer. It is a five-story double tenement

Speculations: Guesses.

house. Already from a distance it gave the impression of not having been repaired for a generation; we did not wish to rely on external impressions, however, but wanted to see with our own eyes what it looks like on the inside, see the rooms in which people live and work, are born and die. Fifteen families live in the house, an average of four on each floor. Each family has a room and a bedroom; the size of the room is 11 by 13 feet, the bedroom 5½ by 7½ feet. In the wall adjoining the dark corridor is a hole measuring 18 inches square, a so-called window; the ceiling height is 7½ feet. Fifty-two people live in this house; moreover the whole bottom floor and half of one of the upper stories are used as an office and a place for packing cigars and as storage space for tobacco and tobacco stems. In two families, four people work in the apartment rooms described above; in three families, three. The remaining families have two workers each but the **strippers** are not included in this figure since this task is usually carried out by an old person who is useless for other occupations or by a child. Tobacco in every stage of preparation is found in all the rooms; mostly it lies spread out over the floor to dry. In the bedroom we find casks, chests, and rusty milk cans that contain tobacco and tobacco stalks, called "stems" by the workers. Working hours are from 6 or 6:30 in the morning until 10, 11, or even 12 o'clock at night. Wages vary from $4.25 to $6.00 [equivalent to $77 to $109 in 2002 prices] in per thousand [cigars rolled] and a family in which two people work can produce 2,800 cigars a week on the average, but the families with more working members do not produce proportionately more, but significantly less for their number. Rent is from $7.00 to $9.00 [$127 to $164] per month. What one finds as furniture in these apartments usually consists first and foremost of a worktable, kitchen table, and cook stove, two or three wooden chairs, a bedstead, and a few cheap pictures of saints. We go through the rooms, the hallway, down the stairs, and into the yard, and everywhere we come across tobacco, tobacco scraps, tobacco stems, and other filth. Even in the yard where the children who are still too young to be able to work—and they have to be very young not to—are playing, great piles of drying tobacco are lying about. One structure in the yard arouses a curious impression; it looks like a small model of a **dilapidated** palace or castle, but when we come nearer our sense of smell quickly tells us what the purpose of this "little palace" is. We go to the door but the stench drives us back; this breeding-ground of disease has no drain to the sewer and consists only of a pit which is emptied out when it is filled to the brim. Great piles of tobacco stems, some 60 to 70 pounds, lie, rotting and moldy,

Strippers: People who prepare tobacco leaves for rolling.

Dilapitated: Run-down.

*in the entry way next to the stairs. We could not ascertain how often these piles are removed to make space for new ones, but the **atrocious** smell emitted by these deposits indicates that it does not happen often. And this odor of tobacco hovers over everything, the infant's cradle, the marriage bed, and the food set before the children. The cellars are dank, damp, and filthy, and the store on the ground floor, which serves as office and packing area, is encrusted with filth. The condition of the upper floors is made even worse by the fact that no water rises to them—and this is the case not only during a period of drought—which, of course, in no way encourages cleanliness. We asked each family that did not regard us with too much suspicion what they thought about efforts to eliminate the tenement factory system and the answer was always the same: "We wish it could be abolished and the sooner the better."...*

ROSENTHAL BROTHERS & Co.

*They own three houses on 15th Street and four on 16th St. No. 623 East 15th St. shelters 20 families numbering 98 people, plus ten people who work there but live elsewhere. Each family has a room of 8 by 10 feet, kitchen of 8 by 6 feet, bedroom of 7 by 5½ feet, ceiling height 7¾ feet. There is only one window in each room in this house, a window 2 feet high and 9 inches wide in the kitchen and an even smaller one in the bedroom, which understandably lets in almost no light or air at all. There is no **hearth** in the whole house, no **mantelpiece**, nothing but a round hole in the chimney through which a stove pipe could be put. In several families three or four people work in one room, surrounded on all sides by huge quantities of tobacco, with the fire blazing with all its might to dry the tobacco sufficiently; obviously under these conditions the air in the rooms is thick and steamy. In one of the rooms the father, mother, and small girl had an eye infection; the mother and a small boy also had sores on their lips. Last week a child died in this house. Rent varies from $7.50 to $8.50 [$136 to $154]; wages are $3.75 [$68] per thousand [cigars]; working hours go from 5 in the morning until 10 or 11 at night. We were told: "We begin around 5 o'clock in the morning and work as long as we can." When calculating the working hours, one must not forget that Sunday is not a day of rest in these tenement factories; most families, despite their religious **scruples**, work until 2 or 3 in the afternoon on Sunday, some the whole day through as on any other day. A family with two workers produces an average of 2,800 cigars per week, provided a third person does the necessary stripping.*

Atrocious: Revolting.

Hearth: Fireplace.

Mantelpiece: The shelf of a fireplace.

Scruples: Principles.

*No. 621 East 15th St. has 18 families, totaling 92 people; 10 others work in the house but do not live there. Seven people were working in an 8-by-8-foot room; two small children were lying in the tobacco. A cookstove was in the room, spreading unbearable heat, next to it a small kitchen table where the family takes its meals. The bedrooms have no windows and neither air nor light can reach them. The room in which this large family works has only one window; the haze and stench are unbearable, the quantity of tobacco enormous, rubbish piled up everywhere. In every way this house resembles the first one we described; a short while ago two children died there of **diarrheal** illnesses....*

*When we went around the corner we came upon the houses owned by the same company on 16th Street; No. 634 is the first with which we wish to acquaint our readers. Sixteen families, consisting of 73 people, live in it; 20 others who do not live in the house work there as well. The families on the street side have a room, kitchen, and bedroom; those who live in the back, only a room and bedroom. The dimensions are: room 10 by 13 feet, kitchen 10 by 9 feet, bedroom 6 by 6½ feet, ceiling height 8 feet. Here as usual we found the only bedroom window 15 inches square looking out on the dark corridor. Six people work in one family and a seventh is hired by it; since last summer four children have died of measles in this house. Great heaps of tobacco lie about the rooms; one is constantly stumbling over tobacco rubbish and stems in the halls and on the steps. Rent varies from $7 to $9 [$127 to $164]. The **water closet** is a drainless **cesspool** full of filth, as are the seats and floors in it.*

No. 636 East 16th St. houses 16 families with 75 people; six people work in the house but do not live there. The ground floor is used as an office; the apartments are the same as at No. 634. Five people work in some families, four in others, two or three in the remainder. Three children have died of diarrheal ailments in this house since last summer. The condition of this house is the same as the earlier one, but it is even dirtier and more dilapidated. The walls, partitions, and stairways are defective and unsafe; the staircase steps are covered with dirt and tobacco refuse. Eight- or nine-year-old children work in several rooms making wrappers; despite its youth, the oldest of these pitiful creatures looks as if it will soon say farewell forever to all work. The water supply is deficient here as well, and the water closets are very filthy....

What we have seen, heard, and smelled so far on our rounds through the atrociously unnatural cigar factories does indeed not

Diarrheal: Intestinal virus.

Water closet: Bathroom.

Cesspool: Underground reservoir for household waste.

encourage us to continue the investigative tour we have begun, and this writer would certainly prefer reporting more pleasant and appetizing things to the reader. But he who has once made it his duty to drag out of its dark hiding place into the light of day the total horror of the system which poisons men, **demeans** *women, and murders children, who has undertaken to show his colleagues, the workers struggling for their daily bread, what a devouring, poisonous cancer the pursuit of the almighty dollar, through* **exploitation, oppression***, and sacrifice of our fellow men, has created in our midst, he must be willing to get his hands dirty in this duty and can say to anyone who turns away, disgusted by the unfolding picture: It is up to us to change it!*

What happened next ...

Samuel Gompers succeeded in organizing cigar makers into a union (an organization of workers that bargains for better pay and working conditions), and in the same year that he wrote his articles about the living conditions of these workers, he organized the Federation of Organized Trades and Labor Unions of the United States and Canada, the forerunner of the American Federation of Labor (AFL). The AFL was a group of unions representing skilled workers (people who had specific skills, such as cigar making) that joined together to push for laws to protect the interests of union members. The AFL was organized by trade, rather than by industry or company. It continues today in the form of the AFL-CIO (American Federation of Labor–Congress of Industrial Organizations), the largest labor organization in the United States.

Despite the efforts of Gompers and others, the use of tenements as factories continued for at least thirty years after Gompers wrote about the cigar makers. From October 1906 to April 1907 a group of consumer groups and organizations opposed to child labor studied the issue in depth and released a report in January 1908. The report concluded that laws banning child labor in factories had been ineffective in eliminating child labor in tenements, which doubled as homes for the workers. Companies that made artificial flow-

While Gompers focused attention on the squalor of tenements, the U.S. Housing Authority suggested a connection between poor neighborhoods and high crime rates, as this poster reflects. *Reproduced by permission of the National Archives and Records Administration.*

ers, for example, continued to rely on home factories to assemble the parts and used children as young as age six to do the work. The fact that work was done in the home instead of in a factory made enforcement of child labor laws difficult.

The 1908 report observed:

> The evils of the system, —intense competition among unskilled workers in a crowded district, low wages, unrestricted hours of work, irregularity of employment, and utilization of

child labor, —are the very conditions which make the system possible and profitable to the employer.... By turning the workers' homes into branches of the factory, he escapes in them the necessity of observing the factory laws.

It was not until 1938 that the Fair Labor Standards Act was passed, establishing both a minimum wage and a minimum age for workers (sixteen years; for hazardous work the minimum age was eighteen). Even so, child labor remains an issue. Underage children of migrant agricultural workers have been found working in the fields, and in developing countries of Asia and Latin America, children still work in U.S.-owned factories, making clothing, athletic shoes, and many other products.

Did you know …

In 1911 Samuel Gompers summarized his goals as a labor union organizer this way:

> Our mission has been the protection of the wage-worker, now; to increase his wages; to cut hours off the long workday, which was killing him; to improve the safety and the sanitary conditions of the workshop; to free him from the tyrannies [severe authority], petty or otherwise, which served to make his existence a slavery.

For more information

Books

Kaufman, Stuart B., ed. *The Samuel Gompers Papers.* Volume 1: *The Making of a Union Leader, 1850–86* (includes "Tenement-House Cigar Manufacture" published in the *New Yorker Volkszeitung,* October 31, 1881). Urbana: University of Illinois Press, 1986.

Livesay, Harold C. *Samuel Gompers and Organized Labor in America.* Prospect Heights, IL: Waveland Press, 1993.

Ranta, Judith A. *Women and Children of the Mills: An Annotated Guide to Nineteenth-Century American Textile Factory Literature.* Westport, CT: Greenwood Press, 1999.

Schlemmer, Bernard, ed., and Philip Dresner, trans. *The Exploited Child.* Paris: L'Institut de Recherche pour le Développement; New York: St. Martin's Press, 2000.

Émile Zola

Excerpts from Germinal

**Published in 1885; translation from
French into English by Havelock Ellis published in 1894**

Coal was the first fuel that ran the Industrial Revolution, the period when machines and factories came into widespread use in manufacturing. The steam engine, which uses the expansive quality of steam to move machinery, requires fuel to heat water to the boiling point, and coal was the most common fuel used for this purpose in the nineteenth century; it continues to be widely used in the twenty-first century. After the first practicable steam engine was introduced in England, in 1772, by James Watt (1736–1819), the demand for coal soared, especially as steam engines were adapted to power trains and ships. For many decades it was also used to heat homes and buildings. Coal provided the basic energy that replaced human muscle power, making it essential to the Industrial Revolution.

Émile Zola (1840–1908) was a French novelist who wrote a series of twenty novels about everyday life in France. *Germinal,* first published in France in 1885, remains one of his best-known works for its representation of the life of the working class, specifically coal miners in northern France. Zola was also known as a social reformer. Working condi-

Émile Zola wrote a series of novels about life in France, including *Germinal*, which describes the working life of coal miners in northern France. *Reproduced by permission of the Library of Congress.*

tions for coal miners (and other workers) in France were not significantly different from those in any other industrialized country, including the United States. Miners were paid poorly and worked in dangerous conditions. *Germinal* conveys the hardships endured by these workers in a way that cold statistics about the working class cannot.

Coal is buried deep inside the Earth (in Zola's novel it is described as being more than two miles below the surface), often embedded in rock, the way the filling of a sandwich is wedged between slices of bread. Once these so-called seams of coal are found, miners dig narrow tunnels to follow them. Miners then use picks or drills to chip away at the coal, and send the coal via carts through the tunnels to vertical mineshafts, where it is hauled to the surface. The tunnels are often just big enough for a man to make his way on his hands and knees, and for the carts to travel back to the mineshaft. Thick boards, called timbers, are placed vertically to support the tunnels, which often are in danger of collapsing, crushing the miners or cutting them off from access to the mineshafts. Other dangers also lurk: a deadly odorless natural gas, called methane, can seep into mines and kill without warning, and underground streams of water can suddenly flood a mine. Miners sometimes took canaries in cages with them into the mines because canaries proved to be sensitive detectors of poisonous gas; if the canaries stopped singing and died, it was an early warning of the presence of methane gas.

Étienne Lantier is a character in *Germinal* who has lost his job working on a railroad and gotten another job working in a coal mine. In this passage, Étienne is descending into the coal mine for the first time. With him are an experienced miner, Maheu, and Maheu's teenage daughter Catherine. Other miners also appear in the story from time to time.

Things to remember while reading the excerpts from *Germinal:*

- Although the story written by Zola is fiction, the conditions he describes were typical of coal mines. Often, entire families, including wives and daughters, worked in the mines. Children often pushed the cars loaded with coal, saving the adults from having to walk doubled over in the low tunnels.

- In Zola's time, coal mine disasters were commonplace. Mining was a very dangerous profession. The disasters hinted at in this passage often did take place, with deadly results. Although safety measures were introduced in the twentieth century, coal mining remains a highly dangerous profession.

- Zola vividly describes the work that took place in a deep coal mine. Some of the terms used in these excerpts, which are translations from the French, may not be clear. The miners enter the mine in "cages," a conveyance something like an elevator but with the sides enclosed by a kind of steel mesh. Cables haul them up and down; at the start of a work shift, the miners wait for empty cages to come up to the surface after delivering the previous load of passengers. Zola describes the mine as a kind of living monster, swallowing the workers and vomiting them later. Inside the mine, miners illuminate the pitch dark with lamps hung on their leather hats (a substitute for a helmet in the nineteenth century), or on buttonholes. At the bottom of the mine, horizontal tunnels go off from the main shaft, leading to other tunnels that are progressively smaller. Small horses, which live inside the mine all the time, are used to haul carts filled with coal to the vertical shaft, where it can be carried to the surface. The temperature inside the mine varies from cold to very hot. Underground water drips constantly, and sometimes seems like rain. For this reason, French miners usually worked barefoot in order to avoid having their shoes become waterlogged.

Excerpt from Germinal, *Chapter 3*

"Golly! It's not warm here," murmured Catherine, shivering.

Étienne contented himself with nodding his head. He was in front of the shaft, in the midst of a vast hall swept by currents of air. He certainly considered himself brave, but he felt a disagreeable emotion at his chest amid this thunder of trains, the hollow blows of the signals, the stifled howling of the trumpet, the continual flight of those cables, unrolled and rolled at full speed by the drums of the engine. The cages rose and sank with the gliding movement of a **nocturnal** beast, always engulfing men, whom the throat of the hole seemed to drink. It was his turn now. He felt very cold, and pre-served a nervous silence which made Zacharie and Levaque [two experienced miners] grin; for both of them disapproved of the hiring of this unknown man [Étienne Lantier], especially Levaque, who was offended that he had not been consulted. So Catherine was glad to hear her father explain things to the young man.

"Look! above the cage there is a parachute with iron **grapnels** to catch into the guides in case of breakage. Does it work? Oh, not always. Yes, the shaft is divided into three compartments, closed by **planking** from top to bottom; in the middle the cages, on the left the passage for the ladders—"

But he interrupted himself to grumble, though taking care not to raise his voice much.

"What are we stuck here for, blast it? What right have they to freeze us in this way?"

The captain, Richomme, who was going down himself, with his **naked** lamp fixed by a nail into the leather of his cap, heard him.

"Careful! Look out for ears," he murmured **paternally**, as an old miner with an affectionate feeling for **comrades**. "Workmen must do what they can. Hold on! here we are; get in with your fellows."

The cage, provided with iron bands and a small-meshed **lattice work**, was in fact awaiting them on the bars. Maheu, Zacharie, and Catherine slid into a **tram** below, and as all five had to enter, Éti-enne in his turn went in, but the good places were taken; he had to squeeze himself near the young girl, whose elbow pressed into his

Nocturnal: Nighttime.

Grapnels: Hooks.

Planking: Heavy, thick boards.

Naked: Unshaded.

Paternally: Father-like.

Comrades: Fellow workers.

Lattice work: Criss-crossed boards.

Tram: A box-like wagon running on rails.

belly. His lamp embarrassed him; they advised him to fasten it to the button-hole of his jacket. Not hearing, he awkwardly kept it in his hand. The **embarkation** continued, above and below, a confused packing of cattle. They did not, however, set out. What, then, was happening? It seemed to him that his impatience lasted for many minutes. At last he felt a shock, and the light grew dim, everything around him seemed to fly, while he experienced the dizzy anxiety of a fall contracting his **bowels**. This lasted as long as he could see light, through the two reception stories, in the midst of the whirling by of the **scaffolding**. Then, having fallen into the blackness of the pit, he became stunned, no longer having any clear perception of his sensations.

"Now we are off," said Maheu quietly.

They were all at their ease. He asked himself at times if he was going up or down. Now and then, when the cage went straight without touching the guides, there seemed to be no motion, but rough shocks were afterwards produced, a sort of dancing amid the **joists**, which made him fear a catastrophe. For the rest he could not distinguish the walls of the shaft behind the lattice work, to which he pressed his face. The lamps feebly lighted the mass of bodies at his feet. Only the captain's naked light, in the neighboring tram, shone like a lighthouse.

"This is four meters [thirteen feet] in diameter," continued Maheu, to instruct him. "The **tubbing** wants doing over again, for the water comes in everywhere. Stop! we are reaching the bottom: do you hear?"

Étienne was, in fact, now asking himself the meaning of this noise of falling rain. A few large drops had at first sounded on the roof of the cage, like the beginning of a shower, and now the rain increased, streaming down, becoming at last a **deluge**. The roof must be full of holes, for a thread of water was flowing on to his shoulder and wetting him to the skin. The cold became icy, and they were buried in black **humidity**, when they passed through a sudden flash of light, the vision of a cavern in which men were moving. But already they had fallen back into darkness.

Maheu said:

"That is the first main level. We are at three hundred and twenty meters [one thousand forty feet]. See the speed."

Raising his lamp he lighted up a joist of the guides which fled by like a rail beneath a train going at full speed; and beyond, as before,

Embarkation: Loading of passengers.

Bowels: Intestines.

Scaffolding: A system of supporting frameworks.

Joists: Vertical timbers.

Tubbing: System to catch water.

Deluge: Downpour.

Humidity: Wetness of the atmosphere.

Young children and adults who worked in coal mines were exposed to many hazards and hardships.
Reproduced by permission of the Library of Congress.

nothing could be seen. They passed three other levels in flashes of light. The deafening rain continued to strike through the darkness.

"How deep it is!" murmured Étienne.

This fall seemed to last for hours. He was suffering for the cramped position he had taken, not daring to move, and especially tortured by Catherine's elbow. She did not speak a word; he only felt her against him and it warmed him. When the cage at last stopped at the bottom, at five hundred and fifty-four meters [eighteen hundred feet], he was astonished to learn that the descent had lasted exactly one minute. But the noise of the bolts fixing themselves, the sensation of solidity beneath, suddenly cheered him; and he was joking when he said to Catherine:

"What have you got under your skin to be so warm? I've got your elbow in my belly, sure enough."

Then she also burst out laughing. Stupid of him, still to take her for a boy! Were his eyes out?

"It's in your eye that you've got my elbow!" she replied, in the midst of a storm of laughter which the astonished young man could not account for.

The cage **voided** its burden of workers, who crossed the pit-eye hall, a chamber cut in the rock, vaulted with masonry, and lighted up by three large lamps. Over the iron flooring the **porters** were violently rolling **laden** trams. A **cavernous** odor exhaled from the walls, a freshness of **saltpetre** in which mingled hot breaths from the neighboring stable. The openings of four **galleries** yawned here.

"This way," said Maheu to Étienne. "You're not there yet. It is still two kilometers [one and a quarter miles]."

The workmen separated, and were lost in groups in the depths of these black holes. Some fifteen went off into that on the left, and Étienne walked last, behind Maheu, who was preceded by Catherine, Zacharie, and Levaque. It was a large gallery for wagons, through a bed of solid rock, which had only needed walling here and there. In single file they still went on without a word, by the tiny flame of the lamps. The young man stumbled at every step, and entangled his feet in the rails. For a moment a hollow sound disturbed him, the sound of a distant storm, the violence of which seemed to increase and to come from the bowels of the earth. Was it the thunder of a **landslip** bringing on to their heads the enormous mass which separated them from the light? A gleam pierced the night, he felt the rock tremble, and when he had placed himself close to the wall, like his comrades, he saw a large white horse close to his face, harnessed to a train of wagons. On the first, and holding the reins, was seated Bébert, while Jeanlin, with his hands leaning on the edge of the last, was running barefooted behind.

They again began their walk. Farther on they reached **crossways**, where two new galleries opened, and the band divided again, the workers gradually entering all the stalls of the mine.

Now the wagon-gallery was constructed of wood; props of timber supported the roof, and made for the crumbly rock a screen of scaffolding, behind which one could see the plates of **schist** glimmering with **mica**, and the coarse masses of dull, rough sandstone. Trains of tubs, full or empty, continually passed, crossing each other with their thunder, borne into the shadow by vague beasts trotting by like phantoms. On the double way of a **shunting** line a long, black serpent slept, a train at standstill, with a snorting horse, whose **crupper** looked like a block fallen from the roof. Doors for

Voided: Emptied.

Porters: Workers responsible for loading coal.

Laden: Loaded.

Cavernous: Cave-like.

Saltpetre: A chemical found in mines.

Galleries: Passageways in a mining system.

Landslip: Shifting earth.

Crossways: An intersection of tunnels.

Schist: A form of rock.

Mica: A mineral that sometimes gleams.

Shunting: A side rail where trains were parked temporarily.

Crupper: Part of a harness.

ventilation were slowly opening and shutting. And as they advanced the gallery became more narrow and lower, and the roof irregular, forcing them to bend their backs constantly.

Étienne struck his head hard; without his leather cap he would have broken his skull. However, he attentively followed the slightest gestures of Maheu, whose **somber** profile was seen against the glimmer of the lamps. None of the workmen **knocked themselves**; they evidently knew each **boss**, each knot of wood or swelling in the rock. The young man also suffered from the slippery soil, which became damper and damper. At times he went through actual puddles, only revealed by the muddy splash of his feet. But what especially astonished him were the sudden changes of temperature. At the bottom of the shaft it was very chilly, and in the wagon-gallery, through which all the air of the mine passed, an icy breeze was blowing, with the violence of a **tempest**, between the narrow walls. Afterwards, as they penetrated more deeply along other passages which only received a meager share of air, the wind fell and the heat increased, a suffocating heat as heavy as lead.

Maheu had not again opened his mouth. He turned down another gallery to the right, simply saying to Étienne, without looking round:

"The Guillaume **seam**."

It was the seam which contained their **cutting**. At the first step, Étienne hurt his head and elbows. The sloping roof descended so low that, for twenty or thirty meters [sixty-five to ninety-seven feet] at a time, he had to walk bent double. The water came up to his ankles. After two hundred meters [two hundred sixteen yards] of this, he saw Levaque, Zacharie, and Catherine disappear, as though they had flown through a narrow **fissure** which was open in front of him.

"We must climb," said Maheu. "Fasten your lamp to a buttonhole and hang on to the wood." He himself disappeared, and Étienne had to follow him. This chimney-passage left in the seam was reserved for miners, and led to all the secondary passages. It was about the thickness of the coal-bed, hardly sixty centimeters [two feet]. Fortunately the young man was thin, for, as he was still awkward, he hoisted himself up with a useless expense of muscle, flattening his shoulders and hips, advancing by the strength of his wrists, clinging to the planks. Fifteen meters [fifty feet] higher they came on the first secondary passage, but they had to continue, as the cutting of Maheu and his mates was in the sixth passage, in

Somber: Serious.

Knocked themselves: Hit their heads.

Boss: Projection.

Tempest: Storm.

Seam: A bed of coal.

Cutting: A straight passage.

Fissure: Crack.

hell, as they said; every fifteen meters [fifty feet] the passages were placed over each other in never-ending succession through this **cleft**, which scraped back and chest. Étienne groaned as if the weight of the rocks had pounded his limbs; with torn hands and bruised legs, he also suffered from lack of air, so that he seemed to feel the blood bursting through his skin. He vaguely saw in one passage two squatting beasts, a big one and a little one, pushing trains: they were Lydie and Mouquette already at work. And he had still to climb the height of two cuttings! He was blinded by sweat, and he despaired of catching up the others, whose **agile** limbs he heard brushing against the rock with a long gliding movement.

"Cheer up! here we are!" said Catherine's voice.

He had, in fact, arrived, and another voice cried from the bottom of the cutting:

"Well, is this the way to treat people? I have two kilometers [one and a quarter miles] to walk from Montsou and I am here first." It was Chaval, a tall, lean, bony fellow of twenty-five, with strongly marked features, who was in a bad humor at having to wait. When he saw Étienne he asked, with **contemptuous** surprise:

"What's that?"

And when Maheu had told him the story he added between his teeth:

"These men are eating the bread of girls."

The two men exchanged, a look, lighted up by one of those instinctive hatreds which suddenly flame up. Étienne had felt the insult without yet understanding it. There was silence, and they got to work. At last all the seams were gradually filled, and the cuttings were in movement at every level and at the end of every passage. The devouring shaft had swallowed its daily ration of men: nearly seven hundred hands, who were now at work in this giant ant-hill, everywhere making holes in the earth, drilling it like an old worm-eaten piece of wood. And in the middle of the heavy silence and crushing weight of the **strata** one could hear, by placing one's ear to the rock, the movement of these human insects at work, from the flight of the cable which moved the cage up and down, to the biting of the tools cutting out the coal at the end of the stalls. Étienne, on turning round, found himself again pressed close to Catherine. But this time he caught a glimpse of the developing curves of her breast: he suddenly understood the warmth which had penetrated him.

Cleft: Division.

Agile: Nimble.

Contemptuous: Disrespectful.

Strata: Layer.

*"You are a girl, then!" he exclaimed, **stupefied**.*

She replied in her cheerful way, without blushing:

"Of course. You've taken your time to find out!"

Excerpt from **Germinal**, *Chapter 4*

*The four **pikemen** had spread themselves one above the other over the whole face of the cutting. Separated by planks, hooked on to retain the fallen coal, they each occupied about four meters [thirteen feet] of the seam, and this seam was so thin, scarcely more than fifty centimeters [one and a half feet] thick at this spot, that they seemed to be flattened between the roof and the wall, dragging themselves along by their knees and elbows, and unable to turn without crushing their shoulders. In order to attack the coal, they had to lie on their sides with their necks twisted and arms raised, **brandishing**, in a sloping direction, their short-handled picks.*

*Below there was, first, Zacharie; Levaque and Chaval were on the stages above, and at the very top was Maheu. Each worked at the **slaty** bed, which he dug out with blows of the pick; then he made two vertical cuttings in the bed and detached the block by burying an iron wedge in its upper part. The coal was rich; the block broke and rolled in fragments along their bellies and thighs. When these fragments, retained by the plank, had collected round them, the pikemen disappeared, buried in the narrow cleft.*

*Maheu suffered most. At the top the temperature rose to thirty-five degrees [ninety-five degrees Fahrenheit], and the air was stagnant, so that in the long run it became lethal. In order to see, he had been obliged to fix his lamp to a nail near his head, and this lamp, close to his skull, still further heated his blood. But his torment was especially aggravated by the moisture. The rock above him, a few centimeters from his face, streamed with water, which fell in large continuous rapid drops with a sort of **obstinate** rhythm, always at the same spot. It was vain for him to twist his head or bend back his neck. They fell on his face, dropping unceasingly. In a quarter of an hour he was soaked, and at the same time covered with sweat, smoking as with the hot steam of a laundry. This morning a drop beating upon his eye made him swear. He would not leave his picking, he dealt great strokes which shook him violently between the two rocks, like a fly caught between two leaves of a book and in danger of being completely flattened.*

Stupified: Astonished.

Pikemen: Miners with picks.

Brandishing: Waving.

Slaty: Covered with slate, a form of rock.

Obstinate: Stubborn.

*Not a word was exchanged. They all hammered; one only heard these irregular blows, which seemed **veiled** and remote. The sounds had a **sonorous** hoarseness, without any echo in the dead air. And it seemed that the darkness was an unknown blackness, thickened by the floating coal dust, made heavy by the gas which weighed on the eyes. The wicks of the lamps beneath their caps of **metallic** tissue only showed as reddish points. One could distinguish nothing. The cutting opened out above like a large chimney, flat and **oblique**, in which the soot of ten years had **amassed** a profound night. **Spectral** figures were moving in it, the gleams of light enabled one to catch a glimpse of a rounded hip, a knotty arm, a vigorous head, **besmeared** as if for a crime. Sometimes, blocks of coal shone suddenly as they became detached, illuminated by a **crystalline** reflection. Then everything fell back into darkness, pickaxes struck great hollow blows; one only heard panting chests, the grunting of discomfort and weariness beneath the weight of the air and the rain of the springs.*

Veiled: Covered.

Sonorous: Loud.

Metallic: Made of metal.

Oblique: Tilted.

Amassed: Collected.

Spectral: Ghostly.

Besmeared: Smeared.

Crystalline: Crystal-like.

What happened next ...

Étienne's first trip into the coal mine suggested all sorts of possible disasters—a mine collapse, a flood, poisonous gas—and in Zola's novel, most of them came to pass. *Germinal* is a harrowing story of the difficulties faced by coal miners in the nineteenth century.

The reality of coal mining was not much different than the novel. In all countries, coal mining was—and still is—a highly dangerous profession. Gradually, though, improved technology and worker demands have resulted in safer conditions for workers.

Moreover, coal-mining techniques have changed significantly. Today, coal operators often scrape the surface of the earth off the top of whole mountains, exposing the coal below. Although this method is safer for miners, it is a technique that greatly concerns environmentalists, since hilltops are stripped of all soil and vegetation and left bare after the coal has been scraped away by gigantic earth-moving machinery.

Did you know ...

In the United States, during the years from 1900 to 2000, there were 104,468 deaths resulting from coal mining accidents. The deadliest year was 1907, when 3,242 miners died. Over that period, the number of coal miners has declined from a high of 862,253 in 1923 to 108,898 in 2000.

For more information

Books

Berg, William J., and Laurey K. Martin. *Emile Zola Revisited*. New York: Twayne Publishers, 1992.

Brown, Frederick. *Zola: A Life*. New York: Farrar, Strauss, Giroux, 1995.

Hemmings, F. W. J. *The Life and Times of Emile Zola*. New York: Scribner, 1977.

Nelson, Brian. *Zola and the Bourgeoisie: A Study of Themes and Techniques in Les Rougon-Macquart*. Totowa, NJ: Barnes and Noble, 1983.

Web Sites

Zola, Émile. *Germinal*. 1885. Translation from French into English by Havelock Ellis published as *Germinal*. New York: Everyman's Library, 1894. *Eldritch Press*. http://209.11.144.65/eldritchpress/ez/germinal. html (accessed on April 11, 2003).

Upton Sinclair

Excerpts from **The Jungle**

Published in 1906

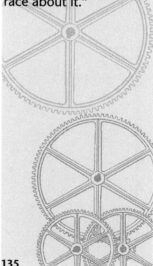

Upton Sinclair (1878–1968) was among a group of writers in the first decade of the twentieth century who were known as muckrakers; the term refers to someone who clears manure from a stall. These writers specialized in writing articles (or, in the case of Sinclair, novels) exposing abuses and wrongdoing by the major business leaders and corporations of the era. They were given their nickname by Theodore Roosevelt (1858–1919), himself a champion of corporate reform.

In 1906 Sinclair published what would turn out to be his most popular novel, *The Jungle*. It tells the story of a family of immigrants from Lithuania who come to Chicago, looking to achieve the American dream of a better life. Instead they find the American nightmare: poverty, death, and despair.

The principal character in the book is Jurgis (YOOR-ghis) Rudkus, a young man from rural Lithuania. Jurgis and his extended family (wife, children, parents-in-law) settle in Chicago. There, the adults in the family get jobs in the city's huge packinghouse industry, where animals are slaughtered and butchered and sent out to stores as food.

"There would be meat stored in great piles in rooms; and the water from leaky roofs would drip over it, and thousands of rats would race about it."

Workers inspect pork innards at a meat-packing plant. Upton Sinclair brought the conditions of such plants into public view in his novel *The Jungle*. *Reproduced by permission of the Library of Congress.*

At first, Jurgis is optimistic. Money is in short supply, but he vows to work harder to earn more. Gradually, however, Jurgis is consumed by his job. He is cheated out of money when buying a house. The horrific working conditions in the packinghouse—wading for hours in cold water, for example—destroy his health and the health of other family members. There is not enough money for a doctor when illness strikes.

The tale of Jurgis's woes was the story Upton Sinclair intended to tell, with the aim of arousing sympathy for the desperately poor workers in Chicago's stockyards (temporary places to keep cattle before they are slaughtered.)

However, in the course of telling the story of Jurgis, Sinclair also told another story: how hogs and cattle were processed and sent to food markets. The book includes graphic descriptions of how packinghouses treated rotten meat with chemicals and packaged it in cans to be sold to unsuspecting consumers. Sinclair described the filthy conditions surrounding the processing of meat, and he wrote of ineffective federal inspectors who were bribed to look the other way and ignore violations of regulations governing sanitation.

It was this consumer aspect of *The Jungle* that captured the nation's attention. The public was outraged to read (even if in a novel) that rotten meat was being repackaged in sausage and in canned products that might end up on the tables of middle-class citizens. In some respects, *The Jungle* was one of the most effective pieces of writing ever published, in terms of arousing the public and causing the federal government to tighten regulations governing the sale of food products.

Things to remember while reading the excerpts from *The Jungle:*

- *The Jungle* is a novel, a work of fiction. But it is based on facts uncovered by Sinclair during nearly two months spent talking to the packinghouse workers in Chicago. Because of the book's realistic treatment of the subject, the public believed that they were reading a factual account of how business was conducted in the stockyards, and they demanded that Congress crack down with tougher rules and tighter inspections.

- Another of Sinclair's themes was the "beef trust," a group of seemingly competitive beef-processing companies that got together to drive up the price of meat. (A trust is a company that owns several other companies in the same industry, with the aim of stifling competition.) Government lawsuits to break up such trusts, and to enforce competition, was a major initiative of President Theodore Roosevelt (see entry), who was in office when *The Jungle* was published.

- The Industrial Revolution (the period when machines and factories came into widespread use in manufacturing) was not limited to the automobile and textile industries. It also extended into agriculture, and especially the processing of animals for food. Prior to the Industrial Revolution, a farmer or rancher might have been responsible for slaughtering and preparing his own animals for a local market (a lack of refrigeration required that most foods were sold near where they were raised). *The Jungle* told how industrial processes had been applied to the food industry, enabling big companies to employ elements of the factory system in raising and slaughtering beef, for example, and distributing foods on a larger scale than was possible before.

- At the beginning of this excerpt, Jurgis Rudkus has just arrived in Chicago, where he will join relatives who arrived earlier from Lithuania. He is taking a tour of Durham's, a giant meatpacking company at which he will soon get a job. Later excerpts, from other chapters, highlight some of his experiences, describing the ways meatpackers created a variety of products—much to the dismay of consumers.

Excerpts from The Jungle

Chapter 3

*Jurgis went down the line with the rest of the visitors, staring openmouthed, lost in wonder. He had **dressed** hogs himself in the forest of Lithuania; but he had never expected to live to see one hog dressed by several hundred men. It was like a wonderful poem to him, and he took it all in **guilelessly**—even to the **conspicuous** signs demanding immaculate cleanliness of the employees. Jurgis was **vexed** when the **cynical** Jokubas translated these signs with sarcastic comments, offering to take them to the secret rooms where the spoiled meats went to be **doctored**....*

*Then the party went across the street to where they did the killing of beef—where every hour they turned four or five hundred cattle into meat. Unlike the place they had left, all this work was done on one floor; and instead of there being one line of **carcasses** which moved to the workmen, there were fifteen or twenty lines, and the men moved from one to another of these. This made a scene of intense activity, a picture of human power wonderful to watch. It was all in one great room, like a circus **amphitheater**, with a **gallery** for visitors running over the center.*

Along one side of the room ran a narrow gallery, a few feet from the floor; into which gallery the cattle were driven by men with

Dressed: Butchered.

Guilelessly: Innocently.

Conspicuous: Obvious.

Vexed: Troubled.

Cynical: Skeptical.

Doctored: Treated.

Carcasses: Bodies of dead animals.

Ampitheater: Arena.

Gallery: A space.

goads which gave them electric shocks. Once crowded in here, the creatures were prisoned, each in a separate pen, by gates that shut, leaving them no room to turn around; and while they stood *bellowing* and plunging, over the top of the pen there leaned one of the "knockers," armed with a sledge hammer, and watching for a chance to deal a blow. The room echoed with the thuds in quick succession, and the stamping and kicking of the steers. The instant the animal had fallen, the "knocker" passed on to another; while a second man raised a lever, and the side of the pen was raised, and the animal, still kicking and struggling, slid out to the "killing bed." Here a man put *shackles* about one leg, and pressed another lever, and the body was jerked up into the air. There were fifteen or twenty such pens, and it was a matter of only a couple of minutes to knock fifteen or twenty cattle and roll them out. Then once more the gates were opened, and another lot rushed in; and so out of each pen there rolled a steady stream of carcasses, which the men upon the killing beds had to get out of the way.

Upton Sinclair, whose novel *The Jungle* details the working conditions of meatpackers in early-twentieth-century Chicago. *Reproduced by permission of AP/Wide World Photos.*

The manner in which they did this was something to be seen and never forgotten. They worked with furious intensity, literally upon the run—at a pace with which there is nothing to be compared except a football game. It was all highly specialized labor, each man having his task to do; generally this would consist of only two or three specific cuts, and he would pass down the line of fifteen or twenty carcasses, making these cuts upon each. First there came the "butcher," to bleed them; this meant one swift stroke, so swift that you could not see it—only the flash of the knife; and before you could realize it, the man had darted on to the next line, and a stream of bright red was pouring out upon the floor. This floor was half an inch deep with blood, in spite of the best efforts of men who kept shoveling it through holes; it must have made the floor slippery, but no one could have guessed this by watching the men at work....

No tiniest particle of *organic* matter was wasted in Durham's. Out of the horns of the cattle they made combs, buttons, hairpins,

Goads: Pointed rods.

Bellowing: Making loud, deep sounds.

Shackles: Restraints.

Organic: Living.

and imitation ivory; out of the shinbones and other big bones they cut knife and toothbrush handles, and mouthpieces for pipes; out of the hoofs they cut hairpins and buttons, before they made the rest into glue. From such things as feet, knuckles, hide clippings, and **sinews** came such strange and unlikely products as **gelatin, isinglass**, and **phosphorus, bone black, shoe blacking**, and **bone oil**. They had curled-hair works for the cattle tails, and a "wool pullery" for the sheepskins; they made **pepsin** from the stomachs of the pigs, and **albumen** from the blood, and violin strings from the ill-smelling **entrails**. When there was nothing else to be done with a thing, they first put it into a tank and got out of it all the **tallow** and grease, and then they made it into fertilizer....

Chapter 5

*It seemed that Antanas Rudkus [Jurgis's father] was working in the room where the men prepared the beef for canning, and the beef had lain in vats full of chemicals, and men with great forks speared it out and dumped it into **trucks**, to be taken to the cooking room. When they had speared out all they could reach, they emptied the vat on the floor, and then with shovels scraped up the balance and dumped it into the truck. This floor was filthy, yet they set Antanas with his mop slopping the **"pickle"** into a hole that connected with a sink, where it was caught and used over again forever; and if that were not enough, there was a trap in the pipe, where all the scraps of meat and odds and ends of refuse were caught, and every few days it was the old man's task to clean these out, and shovel their contents into one of the trucks with the rest of the meat!...*

*One day a man slipped and hurt his leg; and that afternoon, when the last of the cattle had been disposed of, and the men were leaving, Jurgis was ordered to remain and do some special work which this injured man had usually done. It was late, almost dark, and the government inspectors had all gone, and there were only a dozen or two of men on the floor. That day they had killed about four thousand cattle, and these cattle had come in freight trains from far states, and some of them had got hurt. There were some with broken legs, and some with **gored** sides; there were some that had died, from what cause no one could say; and they were all to be disposed of, here in darkness and silence. "Downers," the men called them; and the packinghouse had a special elevator upon which they were raised to the killing beds, where the gang proceeded to handle them, with an air of businesslike **nonchalance** which*

Sinews: Tendons.

Gelatin: A substance used in making jelly.

Isinglass: A substance used to make glue.

Phosphorus: A nonmetallic element.

Bone black: A chemical used in making sugar.

Shoe blacking: Shoe polish.

Bone oil: Substance used as solvent.

Pepsin: A substance used in aiding digestion.

Albumen: A protein found in blood serum.

Entrails: Intestines.

Tallow: Animal fat used to make soap and candles.

Trucks: Hand carts.

Pickle: A solution for cleaning or preserving.

Gored: Wounded.

Nonchalance: Casualness.

*said plainer than any words that it was a matter of everyday routine. It took a couple of hours to get them out of the way, and in the end Jurgis saw them go into the **chilling rooms** with the rest of the meat, being carefully scattered here and there so that they could not be identified. When he came home that night he was in a very **somber** mood, having begun to see at last how those might be right who had laughed at him for his faith in America....*

Chapter 9

*Then one Sunday evening ... Jurgis learned a few things about the great and only Durham canned goods, which had become a national institution. They were regular **alchemists** at Durham's; they advertised a mushroom-catsup, and the men who made it did not know what a mushroom looked like. They advertised "potted chicken,"—and it was like the boardinghouse soup of the comic papers, through which a chicken had walked with **rubbers** on. Perhaps they had a secret process for making chickens chemically—who knows? said Jurgis' friend; the things that went into the mixture were **tripe**,*

Chilling rooms: Large refrigerators.

Somber: Serious.

Alchemists: People who claim to transform common substances into something valuable.

Rubbers: Boots.

Tripe: Stomach tissue.

and the fat of pork, and beef **suet**, and hearts of beef, and finally the waste ends of veal, when they had any. They put these up in several **grades**, and sold them at several prices; but the contents of the cans all came out of the same **hopper**. And then there was "potted game" and "potted grouse," "potted ham," and "deviled ham"—de-vyled, as the men called it. "De-vyled" ham was made out of the waste ends of smoked beef that were too small to be sliced by the machines; and also tripe, dyed with chemicals so that it would not show white; and trimmings of hams and corned beef; and potatoes, skins and all; and finally the hard **cartilaginous gullets** of beef, after the tongues had been cut out. All this **ingenious** mixture was ground up and flavored with spices to make it taste like something. Anybody who could invent a new imitation had been sure of a fortune from old Durham, said Jurgis' **informant**; but it was hard to think of anything new in a place where so many sharp wits had been at work for so long; where men welcomed **tuberculosis** in the cattle they were feeding, because it made them fatten more quickly; and where they bought up all the old **rancid** butter left over in the grocery stores of a continent, and "**oxidized**" it by a forced-air process, to take away the odor, **rechurned** it with skim milk, and sold it in bricks in the cities! Up to a year or two ago it had been the custom to kill horses in the yards—**ostensibly** for fertilizer; but after long agitation the newspapers had been able to make the public realize that the horses were being canned. Now it was against the law to kill horses in **Packingtown**, and the law was really complied with—for the present, at any rate. Any day, however, one might see sharp-horned and shaggy-haired creatures running with the sheep and yet what a job you would have to get the public to believe that a good part of what it buys for lamb and **mutton** is really goat's flesh! ...

With one member trimming beef in a **cannery**, and another working in a sausage factory, the family had a first-hand knowledge of the great majority of Packingtown **swindles**. For it was the custom, as they found, whenever meat was so spoiled that it could not be used for anything else, either to can it or else to chop it up into sausage. With what had been told them by Jonas, who had worked in the pickle rooms, they could now study the whole of the spoiled-meat industry on the inside, and read a new and grim meaning into that old Packingtown jest—that they use everything of the pig except the squeal.

Jonas had told them how the meat that was taken out of pickle would often be found sour, and how they would rub it up with soda

Suet: Animal fat.

Grades: Qualities.

Hopper: Bin.

Cartilaginous gullets: Throats comprising cartilage.

Ingenious: Clever.

Informant: Source of information.

Tuberculosis: A lung disease.

Rancid: Spoiled.

Oxidized: Combined with oxygen.

Rechurned: Stirring again.

Ostensibly: Supposedly.

Packingtown: The area in Chicago where packinghouses were located.

Mutton: Flesh from a mature sheep.

Cannery: Factory for canning food.

Swindles: Dishonest schemes.

to take away the smell, and sell it to be eaten on **free-lunch counters**; also of all the miracles of chemistry which they performed, giving to any sort of meat, fresh or salted, whole or chopped, any color and any flavor and any odor they chose. In the pickling of hams they had an ingenious **apparatus**, by which they saved time and increased the capacity of the plant—a machine consisting of a hollow needle attached to a pump; by plunging this needle into the meat and working with his foot, a man could fill a ham with pickle in a few seconds. And yet, in spite of this, there would be hams found spoiled, some of them with an odor so bad that a man could hardly bear to be in the room with them. To pump into these the packers had a second and much stronger pickle which destroyed the odor—a process known to the workers as "giving them thirty per cent." Also, after the hams had been smoked, there would be found some that had gone to the bad. Formerly these had been sold as "Number Three Grade," but later on some ingenious person had hit upon a new device, and now they would **extract** the bone, about which the bad part generally lay, and insert in the hole a white-hot iron. After this invention there was no longer Number One, Two, and Three Grade—there was only Number One Grade. The packers were always originating such schemes—they had what they called "boneless hams," which were all the odds and ends of pork stuffed into **casings**; and "California hams," which were the shoulders, with big knuckle joints, and nearly all the meat cut out; and fancy "skinned hams," which were made of the oldest hogs, whose skins were so heavy and coarse that no one would buy them—that is, until they had been cooked and chopped fine and labeled "**head cheese!**" ...

Chapter 14

It was only when the whole ham was spoiled that it came into the department of Elzbieta [mother-in-law of Jurgis]. Cut up by the two-thousand-revolutions-a-minute flyers, and mixed with half a ton of other meat, no odor that ever was in a ham could make any difference. There was never the least attention paid to what was cut up for sausage; there would come all the way back from Europe old sausage that had been rejected, and that was moldy and white—it would be **dosed** with **borax** and **glycerine**, and dumped into the hoppers, and made over again for home consumption. There would be meat that had tumbled out on the floor, in the dirt and sawdust, where the workers had tramped and spit uncounted billions of **consumption** germs. There would be meat stored in great piles in rooms; and the water from leaky roofs would drip over it, and thou-

Free-lunch counters: Bars that did not charge customers for food when also ordering beer or whiskey.

Apparatus: Device.

Extract: Take from.

Casings: Membranous materials for processed meat.

Head cheese: A jelly substance made from parts of the head, feet, and other organs of animals.

Dosed: Treated with.

Borox: Cleaning compound.

Glycerine: Chemical used to dissolve fat.

Consumption: Tuberculosis.

*sands of rats would race about on it. It was too dark in these storage places to see well, but a man could run his hand over these piles of meat and sweep off handfuls of the dried **dung** of rats. These rats were nuisances, and the packers would put poisoned bread out for them; they would die, and then rats, bread, and meat would go into the hoppers together. This is no fairy story and no joke; the meat would be shoveled into carts, and the man who did the shoveling would not trouble to lift out a rat even when he saw one—there were things that went into the sausage in comparison with which a poisoned rat was a tidbit. There was no place for the men to wash their hands before they ate their dinner, and so they made a practice of washing them in the water that was to be ladled into the sausage. There were the butt-ends of smoked meat, and the scraps of corned beef, and all the odds and ends of the waste of the plants, that would be dumped into old barrels in the cellar and left there. Under the system of rigid economy which the packers enforced, there were some jobs that it only paid to do once in a long time, and among these was the cleaning out of the waste barrels. Every spring they did it; and in the barrels would be dirt and rust and old nails and stale water—and cartload after cartload of it would be taken up and dumped into the hoppers with fresh meat, and sent out to the public's breakfast. Some of it they would make into "smoked" sausage—but as the smoking took time, and was therefore expensive, they would call upon their chemistry department, and preserve it with borax and color it with gelatine to make it brown. All of their sausage came out of the same bowl, but when they came to wrap it they would stamp some of it "special," and for this they would charge two cents more a pound.*

Dung: Excrement.

What happened next ...

Just months after publication of *The Jungle*, federal legislation was passed mandating improved inspection of meat, as well as requiring labels listing the ingredients of canned food products. The legislation had been proposed years earlier, but a combination of business interests resisted it, arguing that it was not the business of the federal government to regulate what people ate. *The Jungle* demonstrated clearly that people had no way of knowing what was in canned food, and therefore needed government regulation to keep foods safe.

Although women could not vote in 1906, many women were members of clubs that were politically active. They played an important role in persuading the Congress to pass legislation to crack down on abuses in the food industry.

It took longer, however, to address the abuses suffered by workers in the stockyards. Upton Sinclair, who was a socialist, continued to write for decades, constantly promoting laws that would prevent the sort of abuses of poor, unsophisticated workers that he cataloged in *The Jungle*. None of his subsequent works, however, had the impact of this book.

Did you know ...

Prior to the Food and Drug Act, the final passage of which was speeded by *The Jungle,* manufacturers regularly sold "patent medicine" containing ingredients such as opium, morphine, heroin, and cocaine—all dangerous narcotics—without mentioning their presence on product labels. There were no regulations limiting what could be bottled and sold under names such as "Kick-a-poo Indian Sagwa" and "Warner's Safe Cure for Diabetes."

For more information

Books

Hampe, Edward C., Jr., and Merle Wittenberg. *The Lifeline of America; Development of the Food Industry.* New York: McGraw-Hill, 1964.

Jensen, Carl. *Stories That Changed America: Muckrakers of the Twentieth Century.* New York: Seven Stories Press, 2000.

Miller, Walter James. *Upton Sinclair's The Jungle: A Critical Commentary.* New York: Monarch Press, 1983.

Sinclair, Upton. *The Jungle.* New York: Doubleday, Page, and Company, 1906.

Weinberg, Arthur, and Lila Weinberg, eds. *The Muckrakers.* Urbana: University of Illinois Press, 2001.

"Civilization is a method of living and an attitude of equal respect for all people."

Jane Addams

Excerpts from Twenty Years at Hull-House, with Autobiographical Notes

Published in 1910

Jane Addams (1860–1935) is regarded as the first social worker (someone who helps people with a variety of social problems, such as poverty) in the United States. As a young woman she graduated from Rockford College and afterwards decided to pursue a career. Going to college and having a career were both unusual events for women in her era. In the late 1800s, young women were expected to get married and stay at home, but this did not appeal to Addams.

In 1889 she and a college friend, Ellen Gates Starr (1859–1940), founded what came to be called Hull-House. Addams rented an old mansion at the corner of Polk and Halsted Streets in Chicago, a neighborhood filled with recent immigrants from Italy, Russia, Poland, Ireland, Germany, Greece, and Bohemia (a region of today's Czech Republic). She moved her own furniture into the house, and made it available to neighborhood residents, particularly young working-class women.

It was the first so-called settlement house, a place where workers new to the city could find a safe, clean place to stay and to gather. Chicago in the 1880s was in some respects a hostile environment for young women coming from Europe who did not speak English and had little money. Hull-House became a place where they could find day care and a kindergarten for their children, an employment bureau to help them find jobs, as well as a library and classes in art and music.

It also represented an alternative approach to dealing with the social problems, such as unemployment or poverty, created by the rise of large factories filled with machinery, the process known as the Industrial Revolution. Rather than taking a political approach—by campaigning for candidates friendly to working people, for example—Jane Addams took the more personal approach of extending help directly to workers. Hull-House was the core of a reform movement whose participants worked to achieve a long string of improvements, including special courts for juveniles, laws protecting women and children from abuses in factories, and laws regulating the hours and conditions under which children worked. It also established self-help organizations like the Immigrants Protective League, which showed poor workers from other cultures how to help themselves.

Jane Addams is regarded as the first social worker in the United States. *Reproduced by permission of the Library of Congress.*

Things to remember while reading excerpts from *Twenty Years at Hull-House:*

- When Jane Addams and Ellen Starr founded Hull-House, most poor working-class people had few, if any, places to turn for help (with the exception of religious-based charities). Addams was among the first to see that the needs of immigrants extended beyond money and food; they needed help in getting used to a new culture in the United States, help in taking care of babies and small children, and help in becoming educated. Long before business tycoon Andrew Carnegie (see entry) helped pay for building public libraries, Addams established a small public library at Hull-House.

- Addams did not conduct her work without criticism. Her telling of the story of Hull-House includes some gentle jabs at people who mocked her work. For example, she tells of a plan to establish a public bathhouse, where workers could bathe since the homes of many workers lacked indoor plumbing. Some critics, after seeing in some tenements that bathtubs were being used to hold coal (commonly used in stoves to heat houses in the 1880s), concluded that immigrants did not want to bathe. Addams demonstrated that such remarks did not take into account the lack of hot, running water, and ignored the fact that immigrants wanted and needed to bathe just like everyone else.

- Although Addams's main thrust was not politics, she discovered that Hull-House could be useful in organizing local political campaigns aimed at such improvements as, for example, getting streets paved in Chicago's poorer neighborhoods. These small-scale efforts helped demonstrate the power of cooperative action, and made immigrants feel part of American society.

Excerpts from Twenty Years at Hull-House: From Chapter 5, "First Days at Hull-House"

The next January found Miss Starr and myself in Chicago, searching for a neighborhood in which we might put our plans into execution. In our eagerness to win friends for the new undertaking, we utilized every opportunity to set forth the meaning of the Settlement as it had been embodied at **Toynbee Hall***, although in those days we made no appeal for money, meaning to start with our own slender resources. From the very first the plan received courteous attention, and the discussion, while often skeptical, was always friendly. Professor Swing wrote a commendatory column in the* Evening Journal, *and our early speeches were reported quite out of propor-*

Toynbee Hall: A model for Hull-House, established in London in 1884.

tion to their worth. I recall a spirited evening at the home of Mrs. Wilmarth, which was attended by that renowned scholar, **Thomas Davidson,** and by a young Englishman who was a member of the then new **Fabian society** and to whom a peculiar glamour was attached because he had scoured knives all summer in a camp of high-minded philosophers in the **Adirondacks.** Our new little plan met with criticism, not to say disapproval, from Mr. Davidson, who, as nearly as I can remember, called it "one of those unnatural attempts to understand life through cooperative living."

It was in vain we asserted that the collective living was not an essential part of the plan, that we would always **scrupulously** pay our own expenses, and that at any moment we might decide to scatter through the neighborhood and to live in separate **tenements;** he still contended that the fascination for most of those volunteering residence would lie in the collective living aspect of the Settlement. His contention was, of course, essentially sound; there is a constant tendency for the residents to "lose themselves in the cave of their own companionship," as the Toynbee Hall phrase goes, but on the other hand, it is doubtless true that the very companionship, the give and take of colleagues, is what tends to keep the Settlement normal and in touch with "the world of things as they are." I am happy to say that we never resented this nor any other difference of opinion, and that fifteen years later Professor Davidson handsomely acknowledged that the advantages of a group far outweighed the weaknesses he had early pointed out. He was at that later moment sharing with a group of young men, on the East Side of New York, his ripest conclusions in philosophy and was much touched by their intelligent interest and absorbed devotion. I think that time has also justified our early **contention** that the mere **foothold** of a house, easily accessible, ample in space, hospitable and tolerant in spirit, situated in the midst of the large foreign colonies which so easily isolate themselves in American cities, would be in itself a serviceable thing for Chicago. I am not so sure that we succeeded in our endeavors "to make social intercourse express the growing sense of the economic unity of society and to add the social function to democracy." But Hull-House was **soberly** opened on the theory that the dependence of classes on each other is **reciprocal;** and that as the social relation is essentially a reciprocal relation, it gives a form of expression that has peculiar value.

In our search for a vicinity in which to settle we went about with the officers of the compulsory education department, with city missionaries, and with the newspaper reporters whom I recall as a much older set of men than one ordinarily associates with that pro-

Thomas Davidson (1840–1900): A Scottish-American photographer.

Fabian society: A British debating society advocating socialism.

Adirondacks: A mountain chain in New York State.

Scrupulously: Carefully.

Tenements: Houses.

Contention: Belief.

Foothold: Establishment.

Soberly: Seriously.

Reciprocal: Mutual.

The Hull-House building in Chicago provided refuge for many of those who suffered from the more negative consequences of the Industrial Revolution.
Reproduced by permission of AP/Wide World Photos.

Quixotic: Impractical, difficult.

Anarchist: Person who believes in a lack of formal authority/government.

Koerner: Thomas Koerner, nineteenth-century German poet.

Abominable: Unpleasant.

*fession, or perhaps I was only sent out with the older ones on what they must all have considered a **quixotic** mission. One Sunday afternoon in the late winter a reporter took me to visit a so-called **anarchist** Sunday school, several of which were to be found on the northwest side of the city. The young man in charge was of the German student type, and his face flushed with enthusiasm as he led the children singing one of **Koerner's** poems. The newspaperman, who did not understand German, asked me what **abominable** stuff* they were singing, but he seemed dissatisfied with my translation of the simple words and darkly intimated that they were "deep ones," and had probably "fooled" me. When I replied that Koerner was an ardent German poet whose songs inspired his countrymen to resist the aggressions of Napoleon, and that his bound poems were found in the most respectable libraries, he looked at me rather **askance** and I then and there had my first **intimation** that to treat a Chicago man, who is called an anarchist, as you would treat any other citizen, is to lay yourself open to deep suspicion.

Another Sunday afternoon in the early spring, on the way to a **Bohemian** mission in the carriage of one of its founders, we passed a fine old house standing well back from the street, surrounded on three sides by a broad **piazza**, which was supported by wooden pillars of exceptionally pure **Corinthian** design and proportion. I was so attracted by the house that I set forth to visit it the very next day, but though I searched for it then and for several days after, I could not find it, and at length I most reluctantly gave up the search.

Three weeks later, with the advice of several of the oldest residents of Chicago, including the ex-mayor of the city, **Colonel Mason,** who had from the first been a warm friend to our plans, we decided upon a location somewhere near the junction of Blue Island Avenue, Halsted Street, and Harrison Street. I was surprised and overjoyed on the very first day of our search for quarters to come upon the hospitable old house, the quest for which I had so recently abandoned. The house was of course rented, the lower part of it used for offices and storerooms in connection with a factory that stood back of it. However, after some difficulties were overcome, it proved to be possible to **sublet** the second floor and what had been a large drawing-room on the first floor.

The house had passed through many changes since it had been built in 1856 for the homestead of one of Chicago's pioneer citizens, Mr. Charles J. Hull, and although battered by its **vicissitudes,** was essentially sound. Before it had been occupied by the factory, it had sheltered a second-hand furniture store, and at one time the **Little Sisters of the Poor** had used it for a home for the aged. It had a half-skeptical reputation for a haunted attic, so far respected by the tenants living on the second floor that they always kept a large pitcher full of water on the attic stairs. Their explanation of this custom was so **incoherent** that I was sure it was a survival of the belief that a ghost could not cross running water, but perhaps that interpretation was only my eagerness for finding folklore.

Askance: Skeptically.

Intimation: Hint.

Bohemian: A region of what is now the Czech Republic in Europe.

Piazza: Public square.

Corinthian: Ancient Roman.

Colonel Mason: Roswell B. Mason (1805–1892), mayor of Chicago.

Sublet: Rent.

Vicissitudes: Ups and downs.

Little Sisters of the Poor: A Catholic charity.

Incoherent: Hard to understand.

The fine old house responded kindly to repairs, its wide hall and open fireplace always insuring it a gracious aspect. Its generous owner, Miss Helen Culver, in the following spring gave us a free leasehold of the entire house. Her kindness has continued through the years until the group of thirteen buildings, which at present comprises our equipment, is built largely upon land which Miss Culver has put at the service of the Settlement which bears Mr. Hull's name. In those days the house stood between an **undertaking** establishment and a saloon. "Knight, Death and the Devil," the three were called by a Chicago wit, and yet any mock heroics which might be implied by comparing the Settlement to a knight quickly dropped away under the genuine kindness and hearty welcome extended to us by the families living up and down the street.

We furnished the house as we would have furnished it were it in another part of the city, with the photographs and other **impedimenta** we had collected in Europe, and with a few bits of family **mahogany**. While all the new furniture which was bought was enduring in quality, we were careful to keep it in character with the fine old residence. Probably no young **matron** ever placed her own things in her own house with more pleasure than that with which we first furnished Hull-House. We believed that the Settlement may logically bring to its aid all those **adjuncts** which the cultivated man regards as good and suggestive of the best of the life of the past.

On the 18th of September, 1889, Miss Starr and I moved into it, with Miss Mary Keyser, who began performing the housework, but who quickly developed into a very important factor in the life of the vicinity as well as that of the household, and whose death five years later was most sincerely mourned by hundreds of our neighbors.

In our enthusiasm over "settling," the first night we forgot not only to lock but to close a side door opening on Polk Street, and we were much pleased in the morning to find that we possessed a fine illustration of the honesty and kindliness of our new neighbors....

From Chapter 7, "Some Early Undertakings at Hull-House"

At a meeting of working girls held at Hull-House during a strike in a large shoe factory [in which employees refused to work until demands for better pay or conditions were met], the discussions made it clear that the strikers who had been most easily frightened, and therefore first to **capitulate**, were naturally those girls who were

Undertaking: Mortuary.

Impedimenta: Knickknacks.

Mahogany: Wooden furniture.

Matron: A woman in charge of the household affairs of an institution.

Adjuncts: Aspects of life.

Capitulate: Give in.

paying **board** and were afraid of being put out if they fell too far behind. After a recital of a case of peculiar hardship one of them exclaimed: "Wouldn't it be fine if we had a boarding club of our own, and then we could stand by each other in a time like this?" After that events moved quickly. We read aloud together Beatrice Potter's little book on "Cooperation," and discussed all the difficulties and fascinations of such an undertaking, and on the first of May, 1891, two comfortable apartments near Hull-House were rented and furnished. The Settlement was responsible for the furniture and paid the first month's rent, but beyond that the members managed the club themselves. The undertaking "marched," as the French say, from the very first, and always on its own feet. Although there were difficulties, none of them proved **insurmountable**, which was a matter for great satisfaction in the face of a statement made by the head of the **United States Department of Labor**, who, on a visit to the club when it was but two years old, said that his department had investigated many cooperative undertakings, and that none founded and managed by women had ever succeeded. At the end of the third year the club occupied all of the six apartments which the original building contained, and numbered fifty members.

From Chapter 14, "Civic Cooperation"

In our first two summers we had maintained three baths in the basement of our own house for the use of the neighborhood, and they afforded some experience and argument for the erection of the first public bathhouse in Chicago, which was built on a neighboring street and opened under the city Board of Health. The lot upon which it was erected belonged to a friend of Hull-House who offered it to the city without rent, and this enabled the city to erect the first public bath from the small **appropriation** of ten thousand dollars. Great fear was expressed by the public authorities that the baths would not be used, and the old story of the bathtubs in model tenements which had been turned into coal bins was often quoted to us. We were supplied, however, with the **incontrovertible** argument that in our adjacent third square mile there were in 1892 but three bathtubs and that this fact was much complained of by many of the tenement-house dwellers. Our **contention** was justified by the immediate and overflowing use of the public baths, as we had before been sustained in the contention that an immigrant population would respond to opportunities for reading when the Public Library Board had established a branch reading room at Hull-House.

Board: Meals in a rented room.

Insurmountable: Impossible to overcome.

United States Department of Labor: Agency of the federal government.

Appropriation: Public expenditure of funds.

Incontrovertible: Without doubt.

Contention: Argument.

*We also quickly discovered that nothing brought us so absolutely into **comradeship** with our neighbors as mutual and sustained effort such as the paving of a street, the closing of a gambling house, or the restoration of a veteran police sergeant.*

*Several of these earlier attempts at civic cooperation were undertaken in connection with the Hull-House Men's Club, which had been organized in the spring of 1893, had been **incorporated** under a State **charter** of its own, and had occupied a club room in the gymnasium.*

What happened next ...

Many of the goals advocated by Jane Addams eventually were achieved. The practice of social work—extending help to people in need, not only money and food but also counseling and other services—has largely been taken over by government agencies, although private associations like Hull-House continue to play an important role.

Addams's experiments in social reform helped demonstrate the many dimensions of the Industrial Revolution. Although the Industrial Revolution was sparked by technological advances, such as the steam engine and the factory system, it was a "revolution" in the sense that it also profoundly changed the nature of society, giving rise to huge cities where people could not always depend on their individual resources or on family ties to become established.

Did you know ...

Jane Addams did not limit her activities to Hull-House. In 1894 she helped establish the National Federation of Settlements. In 1911 she led the Consumers League and was the first woman president of the National Conference of Charities and Corrections. She also was a vice president of the Campfire Girls and active in the National Child Labor Committee, as well as in the National Association for the Advancement of Colored People and the American Civil Liberties Union. She also found time to campaign actively for women's right to vote.

For more information

Books

Addams, Jane. *Twenty Years at Hull-House, with Autobiographical Notes.* New York: The Macmillan Co., 1910.

Elshtain, Jean Bethke. *Jane Addams and the Dream of American Democracy: A Life.* New York: Basic Books, 2002.

Parks, Deborah A. *Jane Addams: Freedom's Innovator.* Alexandria, VA: Time Life Education, 1999.

Polacheck, Hilda Satt. *I Came a Stranger: The Story of a Hull-House Girl.* Edited by Dena J. Polacheck Epstein. Urbana: University of Illinois Press, 1989.

Polikoff, Barbara Garland. *With One Bold Act: The Story of Jane Addams.* Chicago: Boswell Books, 1999.

Wheeler, Leslie. *Jane Addams.* Englewood Cliffs, NJ: Silver Burdett Press, 1990.

Periodicals

Johnson, Geoffrey. "Sisterhood Was Powerful: The Inspiration for Hull House was Jane Addams's. But She Couldn't Have Pulled Off Her Great Social Experiment without a Little Help from a Friend." *Chicago* 38, (November 1989), p. 192.

Kornblatt, Mark, and Pamela Renner. "'Saint' Jane." *Scholastic Update* 122, (February 23, 1990), p. 10.

Web Sites

Addams, Jane. "Twenty Years at Hull-House with Autobiographical Notes." *University of Pennsylvania: A Celebration of Women Writers.* http://digital.library.upenn.edu/ women/addams/hullhouse/hull-house.html (accessed on April 11, 2003).

"Jane Addams." *About Women's History.* http://womenshistory.about.com/library/bio/blbio_addams.htm (accessed on April 11, 2003).

"Jane Addams—Biography." *Nobel E-Museum.* http://www.nobel.se/peace/laureates/1931/addams-bio.html (accessed on April 11, 2003).

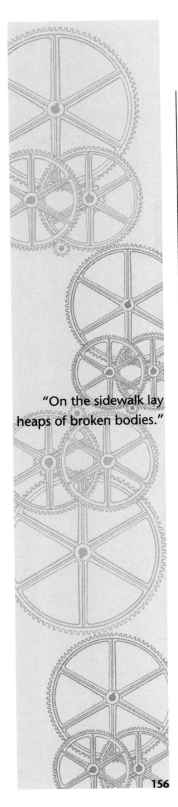

"On the sidewalk lay heaps of broken bodies."

William G. Shepherd

"Eyewitness at the Triangle"

Published in the *Milwaukee Journal*, March 27, 1911

On the afternoon of March 25, 1911, *Milwaukee Journal* reporter William G. Shepherd was walking near the corner of Washington and Greene Streets in lower Manhattan in New York City when he noticed smoke coming from a ten-story building. Reacting with a journalist's instincts, he came closer to watch.

Shepherd picked up a telephone and dictated his story to United Press, which provided news stories via telegraph to newspapers around the country that did not have their own reporters in distant cities.

What Shepherd saw was a fire at the Triangle Shirtwaist Company, which manufactured women's blouses. The company took up the top three floors of the ten-story Asch building. There, about five hundred women, most of them young Jewish immigrants (as young as thirteen), worked at sewing machines. (A shirtwaist is a woman's blouse with a collar designed to look something like a man's shirt. It is worn above a separate skirt.)

Shortly after 4:30 in the afternoon, a fire broke out on the eighth floor, its cause unknown. The volume of loose

fabric in the factory helped the fire spread rapidly. As the women rushed to the freight elevator, stairs, and the fire escape, those on the ninth floor found that the doors had been locked. Then the fire escape collapsed from the weight of so many people on it, eliminating a route to safety.

Firemen were hindered at first by bodies of women who had leapt to their deaths. In addition, fire ladders went only as high as the sixth floor. Firemen held nets for women to jump into, but the netting broke under the impact of several women jumping at the same time.

At the end of the afternoon, it was determined that 146 women had died in just fifteen minutes. Many were killed by leaping through windows and falling to their deaths, as Shepherd's eyewitness account relates. Others were burned to death on the ninth floor. It was the deadliest factory fire in New York history up to that day.

Police attend to victims of the Triangle Shirtwaist Company fire. Many factory owners did not adhere to fire safety regulations and made factories vulnerable to fire. *Reproduced by permission of the Library of Congress.*

Things to remember while reading "Eyewitness at the Triangle":

- At the time of the fire, New York City did not strictly enforce fire safety regulations. Many factory owners resisted the idea of such regulations and questioned the city's right to impose them. Workers in the city were employed in a variety of buildings, including former tenement houses that were vulnerable to the effects of fire.

- The conditions inside the Triangle Shirtwaist Company factory were not unusual for that era. In the decade preceding the deadly fire, the so-called muckrakers (a group of journalists who specialized in uncovering abuses and scandal in industry; see entry) had pointed out dozens of examples of unhealthy, dangerous working conditions. Former President Theodore Roosevelt (1858–1919; in office, 1901–09), who would run in 1912 as the candidate of the Progressive Party (sometimes called the Bull Moose Party; see entry), was one politician who pushed for more government control over businesses.

"Eyewitness at the Triangle"

*I was walking through **Washington Square** when a puff of smoke issuing from the factory building caught my eye. I reached the building before the alarm was turned in. I saw every feature of the tragedy visible from outside the building. I learned a new sound—a more horrible sound than description can picture. It was the thud of a speeding, living body on a stone sidewalk.*

Thud—dead, thud—dead, thud—dead, thud—dead. Sixty-two thud—deads. I call them that, because the sound and the thought of death came to me each time, at the same instant. There was plenty of chance to watch them as they came down. The height was eighty feet.

The first ten thud—deads shocked me. I looked up—saw that there were scores of girls at the windows. The flames from the floor below were beating in their faces. Somehow I knew that they, too,

Washington Square: A park in Manhattan, one of the five boroughs of New York City.

must come down, and something within me—something that I didn't know was there—steeled me.

I even watched one girl falling. Waving her arms, trying to keep her body upright until the very instant she struck the sidewalk, she was trying to balance herself. Then came the thud—then a silent, unmoving pile of clothing and twisted, broken limbs.

As I reached the scene of the fire, a cloud of smoke hung over the building.... There was a living picture in each window—four screaming heads of girls waving their arms.

Members of several garment workers unions gather in the aftermath of the Triangle Shirtwaist Company fire in New York City. *Reproduced by permission of AP/Wide World Photos.*

William G. Shepherd   159

"Call the firemen," they screamed—scores of them. "Get a ladder," cried others. They were all as alive and whole and sound as were we who stood on the sidewalk. I couldn't help thinking of that. We cried to them not to jump. We heard the siren of a fire engine in the distance. The other sirens sounded from several directions.

"Here they come," we yelled. "Don't jump; stay there."

One girl climbed onto the window sash. Those behind her tried to hold her back. Then she dropped into space. I didn't notice whether those above watched her drop because I had turned away. Then came that first thud. I looked up, another girl was climbing onto the window sill; others were crowding behind her. She dropped. I watched her fall, and again the dreadful sound. Two windows away two girls were climbing onto the sill; they were fighting each other and crowding for air. Behind them I saw many screaming heads. They fell almost together, but I heard two distinct thuds. Then the flames burst out through the windows on the floor below them, and curled up into their faces.

The firemen began to raise a ladder. Others took out a life net and, while they were rushing to the sidewalk with it, two more girls shot down. The firemen held it under them; the bodies broke it; the grotesque simile of a dog jumping through a hoop struck me. Before they could move the net another girl's body flashed through it. The thuds were just as loud, it seemed, as if there had been no net there. It seemed to me that the thuds were so loud that they might have been heard all over the city.

I had counted ten. Then my dulled senses began to work automatically. I noticed things that it had not occurred to me before to notice. Little details that the first shock had blinded me to. I looked up to see whether those above watched those who fell. I noticed that they did; they watched them every inch of the way down and probably heard the roaring thuds that we heard.

As I looked up I saw a love affair in the midst of all the horror. A young man helped a girl to the window sill. Then he held her out, deliberately away from the building and let her drop. He seemed cool and calculating. He held out a second girl the same way and let her drop. Then he held out a third girl who did not resist. I noticed that. They were as unresisting as if he were helping them onto a streetcar instead of into eternity. Undoubtedly he saw that a terrible death awaited them in the flames, and his was only a terrible chivalry.

Then came the love amid the flames. He brought another girl to the window. Those of us who were looking saw her put her arms

Sash: Frame.

Grotesque simile: Disturbing comparison.

Chivalry: Marked by special consideration.

about him and kiss him. Then he held her out into space and dropped her. But quick as a flash he was on the window sill himself. His coat fluttered upward—the air filled his trouser legs. I could see that he wore tan shoes and **hose.** His hat remained on his head.

Thud—dead, thud—dead—together they went into eternity. I saw his face before they covered it. You could see in it that he was a real man. He had done his best.

We found out later that, in the room in which he stood, many girls were being burned to death by the flames and were screaming in an inferno of flame and heat. He chose the easiest way and was brave enough to even help the girl he loved to a quicker death, after she had given him a goodbye kiss. He leaped with an energy as if to arrive first in that mysterious land of eternity, but her thud—dead came first.

The firemen raised the longest ladder. It reached only to the sixth floor. I saw the last girl jump at it and miss it. And then the faces disappeared from the window. But now the crowd was enormous, though all this had occurred in less than seven minutes, the start of the fire and the thuds and deaths.

I heard screams around the corner and hurried there. What I had seen before was not so terrible as what had followed. Up in the [ninth] floor girls were burning to death before our very eyes. They were jammed in the windows. No one was lucky enough to be able to jump, it seemed. But, one by one, the jams broke. Down came the bodies in a shower, burning, smoking—flaming bodies, with **disheveled** hair trailing upward. They had fought each other to die by jumping instead of by fire.

The whole, sound, unharmed girls who had jumped on the other side of the building had tried to fall feet down. But these fire torches, suffering ones, fell **inertly**, only intent that death should come to them on the sidewalk instead of in the furnace behind them.

On the sidewalk lay heaps of broken bodies. A policeman later went about with tags, which he fastened with wires to the wrists of the dead girls, numbering each with a lead pencil, and I saw him fasten tag no. 54 to the wrist of a girl who wore an engagement ring. A fireman who came downstairs from the building told me that there were at least fifty bodies in the big room.... Another fireman told me that more girls had jumped down an air shaft in the rear of the building. I went back there, into the narrow court, and saw a heap of dead girls....

Hose: Twin socks.

Disheveled: Uncombed.

Inertly: Without motion.

The floods of water from the firemen's hose that ran into the
gutter were actually stained red with blood. I looked upon the heap
of dead bodies and I remembered these girls were the shirtwaist
makers. I remembered their great strike of last year in which these
same girls had demanded more sanitary conditions and more safety
precautions in the shops. These dead bodies were the answer.

What happened next ...

The Triangle Shirtwaist factory fire shocked much of the country. In New York City, an investigation resulted in creation of a Bureau of Fire Investigation, which was given power to require more safety measures in workplaces. Nevertheless, the commission stopped short of taking all the recommended steps, partly on grounds that it would cost factory owners too much money.

The families of twenty-three victims sued the Triangle Shirtwaist Company and eventually were paid seventy-five dollars each (a sum worth just under fourteen hundred dollars in 2003).

The Triangle Shirtwaist fire became a rallying cry for labor unions (worker organizations that bargained with employers for higher pay and better working conditions). After the fire, many garment workers joined the International Ladies Garment Workers Union, which demanded that factory owners assure safer working conditions, as well as higher pay.

Did you know ...

Each year on March 25, the International Ladies Garment Workers Union holds a memorial at the site of the fire.

For more information

Books

Shepherd, William G. "Eyewitness at the Triangle." *Milwaukee Journal*, March 27, 1911.

Stein, Leon. *The Triangle Fire*. Philadelphia, PA: J. B. Lippincott, 1962.

Tyler, Gus. *Look for the Union Label: A History of the International Ladies' Garment Workers' Union*. Armonk, NY: M.E. Sharpe, 1995.

Periodicals

Gould, Stephen Jay. "A Tale of Two Worksites." *Natural History* 106, no. 9, October 1997, p. 18.

Web Sites

"The Triangle Factory Fire." *The Kheel Center at the Cornell University Library.* http://www.ilr.cornell.edu/trianglefire/ (accessed on April 11, 2003).

Camella Teoli

Excerpt from U.S. Congressional Hearings, March 2–7, 1912

Reproduced in Joyce Kornbluh's *Rebel Voices: An I.W.W. Anthology,* published in 1964

When Camella Teoli was in the seventh grade, she did not go to school. She went to work in a factory.

Children had been employed in textile factories ever since textile factories were first built in Britain during the last part of the 1700s. Children made ideal workers: they did not complain about low wages or long hours, they did not argue with overseers, and they were small and nimble—their tiny hands were ideal for operating textile machines.

As with adult workers, children were sometimes injured on the job. Sometimes their injuries resulted in death; other times, they were maimed or crippled for life. In both Britain and the United States, these incidents eventually led to laws barring very young children from working in factories. Most factory owners resisted such laws because it was highly profitable to employ children, who were paid less than adults were.

Child labor laws did not always stop factory owners from employing younger children, as was the case with Camella Teoli. She became known following a famous strike in Lawrence, Massachusetts, in 1913. Lawrence was an impor-

tant center of textile mills at the time and there was always a demand for workers to keep the factories humming.

In 1912 textile workers in Lawrence went on strike (refused to work) to protest a reduction in their pay imposed by the city's largest textile mill, the American Woolen Company. A state law had gone into effect on January 1, 1912, requiring a shorter workweek. American Woolen responded by reducing workers' pay in proportion to the reduction in hours worked. In response, the workers refused to work until their pay was restored to its former level. Strikes were not new in 1913, but unlike most strikes, which involved men, more than half the workers at American Woolen were women and children under age eighteen, most of whom were recent immigrants to the United States from Europe.

Police and militiamen (soldiers) were called to maintain order, although some critics thought the show of force was meant to discourage strikers. After some parents of children who worked at the mill tried to send their children out of town—for safety and to be sure they could not go to work—police tried to prevent other such children from leaving the city. As in many strikes, violence did break out (each side blamed the other for starting it), and at least two deaths resulted. These deaths, and the fact that many of the strikers were women and children, drew widespread attention in newspapers. In March 1912 the U.S. Congress called hearings to investigate the circumstances of the strike and the reaction of local authorities.

Things to remember while reading the excerpt from U.S. Congressional Hearings:

- Camella Teoli was the daughter of an Italian immigrant. Her life was similar to the lives of many immigrants in the period 1890–1920. Poor and unsophisticated, they worked long hours for low wages. In some cases, parents sent young children to work to earn money despite a Massachusetts law requiring workers to be at least fourteen. In her interview at the Congressional hearing, Teoli testifies about a man who was looking for mill workers; he volunteered to get a false document stating that Teoli was fourteen years old and therefore eligible to work in the mill. (Her father thought she might be only thirteen at the time; documents like a birth certificate were not commonly held by immigrants at the time.) The existence of a man going around town looking for young workers demonstrated how factories needed to find workers in much the same way they needed to find supplies of wool or cotton to make cloth. Both were required to keep the mills running and the profits growing.

- The strike against the American Woolen Company was organized by the Industrial Workers of the World (IWW),

The Lawrence Textile Strike of 1912

On January 1, 1912, a Massachusetts law went into effect reducing the workweek from fifty-six hours to fifty-four hours. In response, textile mills in Lawrence, Massachusetts, reduced the wages paid to their workers, primarily young women and girls. The reduction was the equivalent of two hours of work a week. A bill designed to improve the condition of workers was made to cost them money instead.

On January 12, ten thousand workers went on strike in Lawrence, led by the Industrial Workers of the World (IWW), a labor organization that concentrated on organizing so-called unskilled workers—people who lacked traditional skills like weaving or carpentry and who were usually the lowest paid workers. The strike lasted for a little over two months and was characterized by violent encounters between, on one side, Massachusetts state militiamen (similar to the National Guard) and city policemen, (brought in to keep order and protect the factory from vandalism), and, on the other side, the mostly female strikers.

One technique used in the strike raised particular interest. Strikers decided to send their children out of town to stay with relatives or workers sympathetic with the aims of the strike. In this way, the children were made unavailable to work in the factory. After one trainload of so-called strike waifs left without incident, the Lawrence police chief blocked other children from leaving the city. He argued that he needed proof that the children were really being sent away by their parents, rather than by the Industrial Workers of the World.

In mid-March 1912, the U.S. Congress held hearings about the strike, and invited several strikers to appear. Once the strike—and the testimony of strikers before Congress—gained national attention, the cause of the strikers was assured. The mill owners agreed to most of the demands of the striking women, notably restoration of their pay. The strikers were victorious.

The strike was later viewed by historians as a landmark not only for the efforts of unions to gain power, but also in the history of women, who at the time were still seven years away from achieving the right to vote.

a labor organization that organized workers in an effort to improve their pay and working conditions. The involvement of the IWW, whose members were known as Wobblies, was one of the aspects of the strike that drew the public's attention, as the organization advocated policies (such as government control over factories) regarded as dangerous by most politicians and especially by employers. On the other hand, the strikers, young women and children, aroused sympathy among the public.

- While all wages paid to textile workers in 1912 were low, the dollar amounts mentioned in this testimony seem especially low compared to wages in 2003. The wages that appear in brackets after dollar amounts mentioned in the article are updated to reflect the value of a dollar in 2003. For example, Teoli said she earned $6.55 [$119 per week]. This means that $6.55 in 1912 would be roughly the same as being paid $119 in 2003. Put another way, she was paid about $2.20 an hour in 2003 dollars, or roughly one-third of the legal minimum wage in 2003.

- Toward the end of the questioning, Teoli's answers indicate that she does not know or cannot remember all of the details of the situation. Was this because she was ignorant of these facts, or because she was fearful of answering the questions, perhaps afraid she would get in trouble with the congressmen or with her father. The testimony does not answer this question, but it hints at how pressure could be put on children to do their jobs without complaining.

Excerpt from U.S. Congressional Hearings

THE CHAIRMAN: Camella, how old are you?

MISS TEOLI: Fourteen years and eight months.

THE CHAIRMAN: Fourteen years and eight months?

MISS TEOLI: Yes.

THE CHAIRMAN: How many children are there in your family?

MISS TEOLI: Five.

THE CHAIRMAN: Where do you work?

MISS TEOLI: In the woolen mill.

THE CHAIRMAN: For the American Woolen Co.?

MISS TEOLI: Yes.

THE CHAIRMAN: What sort of work do you do?

MISS TEOLI: *Twisting*.

THE CHAIRMAN: You do twisting?

MISS TEOLI: Yes.

THE CHAIRMAN: How much do you get a week?

MISS TEOLI: $6.55 [$119 in 2003 prices].

THE CHAIRMAN: What is the smallest pay?

MISS TEOLI: $2.64 [$47.96].

THE CHAIRMAN: Do you have to pay anything for water [to drink at work]?

MISS TEOLI: Yes.

THE CHAIRMAN: How much?

MISS TEOLI: 10 cents [$1.80] every two weeks.

THE CHAIRMAN: Do they hold back any of your pay?

MISS TEOLI: No.

THE CHAIRMAN: Have they ever held back any?

MISS TEOLI: One week's pay.

THE CHAIRMAN: They have held back one week's pay?

MISS TEOLI: Yes.

THE CHAIRMAN: Does your father work, and where?

MISS TEOLI: My father works in the Washington.

THE CHAIRMAN: The Washington Woolen Mill [in Lawrence]?

MISS TEOLI: Yes, sir.

THE CHAIRMAN: How much pay does he get for a week's work?

MISS TEOLI: $7.70 [$139.90].

THE CHAIRMAN: Does he always work a full week?

MISS TEOLI: No.

THE CHAIRMAN: Well, how often does it happen that he does not work a full week?

MISS TEOLI: He works in the winter a full week, and usually he don't in the summer.

THE CHAIRMAN: In the winter he works a full week, and in the summer how much?

MISS TEOLI: Two or three days a week.

Twisting: Spinning yarn from wool.

A young girl stands in front of a power loom at a textile factory. Many children who were below the legal age of working were hired by factory owners. *Reproduced by permission of the National Archives and Records Administration.*

THE CHAIRMAN: What sort of work does he do?

MISS TEOLI: He is a **comber**.

THE CHAIRMAN: Now, did you ever get hurt in the mill?

MISS TEOLI: Yes.

THE CHAIRMAN: Can you tell the committee about that—how it happened and what it was?

MISS TEOLI: Yes.

THE CHAIRMAN: Tell us about it now, in your own way.

MISS TEOLI: Well, I used to go to school, and then a man came up to my house and asked my father why I didn't go to work, so my father says I don't know whether she is 13 or 14 years old. So, the man say you give me $4 [$72.50] and I will make the papers come from the old country saying you are 14. So, my father gave him the $4 [$72.50], and in one month came the papers that I was 14. I went to work, and about two weeks got hurt in my head.

Comber: A worker who combs wool before it is fed into a spinning machine.

THE CHAIRMAN: Now, how did you get hurt, and where were you hurt in the head; explain that to the committee?

MISS TEOLI: I got hurt in Washington.

THE CHAIRMAN: In the Washington Mill?

MISS TEOLI: Yes, sir.

THE CHAIRMAN: What part of your head?

MISS TEOLI: My head.

THE CHAIRMAN: Well, how were you hurt?

MISS TEOLI: The machine pulled the scalp off.

THE CHAIRMAN: The machine pulled your scalp off?

MISS TEOLI: Yes, sir.

THE CHAIRMAN: How long ago was that?

MISS TEOLI: A year ago, or about a year ago.

THE CHAIRMAN: Were you in the hospital after that?

MISS TEOLI: I was in the hospital seven months.

THE CHAIRMAN: Seven months?

MISS TEOLI: Yes.

THE CHAIRMAN: Did the company pay your bills while you were in the hospital?

MISS TEOLI: Yes, sir.

THE CHAIRMAN: The company took care of you?

MISS TEOLI: The company only paid my bills; they didn't give me anything else.

THE CHAIRMAN: They only paid your hospital bills; they did not give you any pay?

MISS TEOLI: No, sir.

THE CHAIRMAN: But paid the doctors' bills and hospital fees?

MISS TEOLI: Yes, sir.

MR. LENROOT (Representative Irvine L. Lenroot from Wisconsin): They did not pay your wages?

MISS TEOLI: No, sir.

THE CHAIRMAN: Did they arrest your father for having sent you to work at 14?

MISS TEOLI: Yes, sir.

THE CHAIRMAN: What did they do with him after they arrested him?

MISS TEOLI: My father told this about the man he gave $4 [$72.50] to, and then they put him on [the job] again.

THE CHAIRMAN: Are you still being treated by the doctors for the scalp wound?

MISS TEOLI: Yes, sir.

THE CHAIRMAN: How much longer do they tell you [that] you will have to be treated?

MISS TEOLI: They don't know.

THE CHAIRMAN: They do not know?

MISS TEOLI: No.

THE CHAIRMAN: Are you working now?

MISS TEOLI: Yes, sir.

THE CHAIRMAN: How much are you getting?

MISS TEOLI: $6.55 [$119].

THE CHAIRMAN: Are you working in the same place where you were before you were hurt?

MISS TEOLI: No.

THE CHAIRMAN: In another mill?

MISS TEOLI: Yes.

THE CHAIRMAN: What mill?

MISS TEOLI: The Wood Mill.

THE CHAIRMAN: The what?

MISS TEOLI: The Wood Mill.

THE CHAIRMAN: Were you down at the station on Saturday, the 24th of February [the occasion of a violent incident]?

MISS TEOLI: I work in a town in Massachusetts, and I don't know nothing about that.

THE CHAIRMAN: You do not know anything about that?

MISS TEOLI: No, sir.

THE CHAIRMAN: How long did you go to school?

MISS TEOLI: I left when I was in the sixth grade.

THE CHAIRMAN: You left when you were in the sixth grade?

MISS TEOLI: Yes, sir.

THE CHAIRMAN: And you have been working ever since, except while you were in the hospital?

MISS TEOLI: Yes, sir.

MR. CAMPBELL [Representative Philip Campbell of Kansas]: Do you know the man who came to your father and offered to get a certificate that you were 14 years of age?

MISS TEOLI: I know the man, but I have forgot him now.

MR. CAMPBELL: You know him, but you do not remember his name now?

MISS TEOLI: Yes.

MR. CAMPBELL: Do you know what he did; what his work was?

MISS TEOLI: No.

MR. CAMPBELL: Was he connected with any of the mills?

MISS TEOLI: I don't know.

MR. CAMPBELL: Is he an Italian?

MISS TEOLI: Yes, sir.

MR. CAMBELL: He knew your father well?

MISS TEOLI: Yes, sir.

MR. CAMPBELL: Was he a friend of your father?

MISS TEOLI: No.

MR. CAMPBELL: Did he ever come about your house visiting there?

MISS TEOLI: I don't know.

MR. CAMPBELL: I mean before he asked about your going to work in the mills?

MISS TEOLI: Yes, sir.

MR. CAMPBELL: He used to come to your house and was a friend of the family?

MISS TEOLI: Yes.

MR. CAMPBELL: You are sure he was not connected or employed by some of the mills?

MISS TEOLI: I don't know, I don't think so.

MR. CAMPBELL: Do they go around in Lawrence there and find little girls and boys in the schools over 14 years of age and urge them to quit school and go to work in the mills?

MISS TEOLI: I don't know.

MR. CAMPBELL: You don't know anything about that?

MISS TEOLI: No.

MR. CAMPBELL: Do you know of any little girls besides yourself, who were asked to go to work as soon as they were 14?

MISS TEOLI: No, I don't know; no.

MR. HARDWICK [Representative Thomas Harwick of Georgia]: Are you one of the strikers?

MISS TEOLI: Yes, sir.

What happened next ...

The strike was a public relations disaster for the American Woolen Company. At the end of March 1912, the company agreed to almost all the strikers' demands, including restoration of their previous pay, and the workers returned to their jobs. Perhaps more significantly, many of the workers in the Lawrence strike had no specific skills—many were employed to tend to the textile machines—and their success marked the beginning of demands by unskilled workers to achieve a minimum standard of living enjoyed by skilled workers.

Although the strikers in Lawrence won their strike, it was just one battle in a long struggle by workers in the textile industry. Only a handful of textile mills still operate in Lawrence, a city once filled with mills. Over the years, many owners shut down their mills in Massachusetts and opened new ones in other states, notably in the South, where workers were less likely to be union members and could be hired for lower wages. Still later, mills moved outside the United States to less developed countries of Latin America or East Asia, where workers could be hired for even lower wages.

Did you know ...

The Lawrence textile strike became known as the "Bread and Roses Strike." The name comes from the idea that the strikers were fighting not only for money to buy food (bread), but also for a more decent life (roses) that was not limited to an endless round of work, sleep, and more work.

The testimony of Camella Teoli received added attention because first lady Helen Herron Taft—wife of President William Howard Taft (1857–1930)—was in the audience.

For more information

Books

Conlin, Joseph Robert. *Bread and Roses Too: Studies of the Wobblies.* Westport, CT: Greenwood, 1969.

Dubofsky, Melvyn. *We Shall Be All: A History of the Industrial Workers of the World.* 2nd ed. Urbana: University of Illinois Press, 1988.

Kornbluh, Joyce L., ed. *Rebel Voices: An I.W.W. Anthology.* Ann Arbor: University of Michigan Press, 1964.

Werstein, Irving. *Pie in the Sky, an American Struggle: The Wobblies and Their Times.* New York: Delacorte Press, 1969.

Web Sites

Dublin, Thomas, and Kerri Harney. "The 1912 Lawrence Strike: How Did Immigrant Workers Struggle to Achieve an American Standard of Living?" *Women and Social Movements in the United States, 1775–2000.* http://womhist.binghamton.edu/law/intro.htm (accessed on April 11, 2003).

Politics and Law

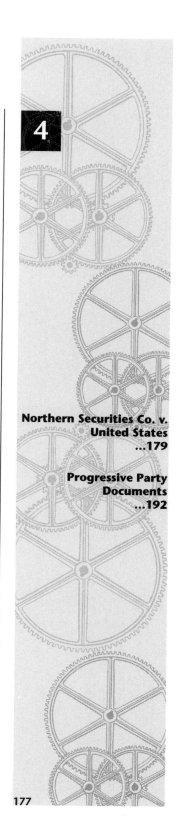

For many years after the first steam- or water-powered machines were installed in English textile factories in the second half of the eighteenth century, most government leaders believed they had no legitimate business interfering with private individuals conducting their business.

But as the nineteenth century wore on, evidence mounted that many workers, especially children, were being abused in factories by being forced to work long hours for low pay and under dangerous, unhealthy conditions. Slowly, advocates of workers' rights succeeded in passing laws that regulated how many hours children could be forced to work, and established a minimum age for factory employees.

At the end of the nineteenth century, attitudes toward the business practices of some owners also came under scrutiny. The government of President Theodore Roosevelt (1858–1919) in particular advocated government action to make sure that a few large business owners did not stifle competition and raise prices for everyone. Roosevelt was part of what was called the Progressive movement, the notion that government regulation was required as a counterbalance to the immense economic power of the very large businesses, such as the Standard Oil Company, owned by John D. Rockefeller (1839–1937). The Progressives acted both through politics, by running for office, and through the courts, by enforcing federal laws that barred monopolies (companies that controlled whole industries through a complex web of corporate ownership called trusts).

In 1904, one such monopoly, the Northern Securities Company, was taken to court by the government of President Roosevelt. The suit claimed that the firm, which had been organized to acquire stock in two railroads, the Northern Pacific and the Great Northern, violated the 1890 Sherman Antitrust Act and effectively discouraged competition from other railroads in the northern part of the United States. The U.S. Supreme Court ruled in favor of the government, and Northern Securities, owned by J. P. Morgan (1837–1913) and James J. Hill (1838–1916), was forced to break up.

Although Roosevelt stepped away from the national scene after his second term ended in 1909, he returned to presidential politics in 1912. Unhappy with the performance of his hand-picked successor, William Howard Taft (1857–1930), Roosevelt ran against him in the Republican primaries, but lost. Undeterred, Roosevelt ran as the third-party candidate of the Progressive Party, also known as the Bull Moose Party. The party's platform and Roosevelt's acceptance speech highlight the continuation of the Progressive movement.

Northern Securities Co.
v. United States

Excerpt from the United States Supreme Court decision

1904

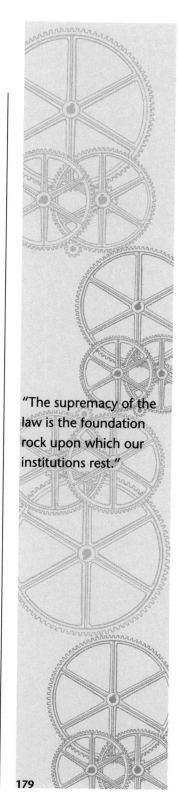

In 1904 the U.S. Supreme Court ruled that the federal government had the right to break up a corporation called the Northern Securities Company. The company had been organized in November 1901 by Wall Street banker J. Pierpont Morgan (1837–1913) and railroad owner James J. Hill (1838–1916). The purpose of the new company was to acquire stock in two railroads, the Northern Pacific and the Great Northern. Both ran trains across the northern part of the United States, from the Great Lakes in the East to Puget Sound (near Seattle) in the West.

The government of President Theodore Roosevelt (1858–1919) filed suit to break up Northern Securities, on the grounds that such a company violated the 1890 Sherman Antitrust Act. The government argued that simply by forming a company that owned stock in two competing railroads (one of which, the Northern Pacific, was bankrupt), Morgan and Hill would be acting to discourage competition in the railroad business in the northern part of the country. The Sherman Antitrust Act was designed to prevent that very thing. (A trust was a corporation whose purpose was to own stock

> "The supremacy of the law is the foundation rock upon which our institutions rest."

in other companies within the same industry; by owning many companies in the same industry, trusts were a way of controlling, or avoiding, competition.)

The owners of Northern Securities fought the government's lawsuit. They claimed that the federal government had no right under the U.S. Constitution to regulate the purchase of stocks in a company; instead, the companies told the Supreme Court, that right belonged to state governments. Since the Northern Securities Company had been formed under the laws of New Jersey, the federal government had no legal power to stop it. The company's lawyers also argued that there was a difference between conducting interstate commerce (business between states), which the federal government had the Constitutional power to regulate, and the act of buying or selling shares in a railroad company.

J. P. Morgan (pictured) and James J. Hill were accused by the U.S. government of violating the Sherman Antitrust Act. *Reproduced by permission of the Corbis Corporation.*

In effect, the legal argument that reached the Supreme Court in December 1903 was about the power of the federal government to regulate companies. President Roosevelt believed that the federal government should act forcefully to control companies that threatened to discourage competition and thereby drive up prices or force other companies to follow orders. President Roosevelt believed that only the federal government was large enough to exert control over giant firms that came into existence toward the end of the nineteenth century.

On the other side, Morgan and Hill argued that the powers of the federal government were limited by the Constitution, and that rules about interstate commerce could not be extended to the act of simply owning property (as opposed to operating a company). Viewed in this light, the Supreme Court case dealt with a basic issue: the rights of private property owners versus the rights of a democratically elected government.

The Supreme Court was divided, five to four, in its decision. The majority of the Court's nine justices ruled in favor of the government, saying in their opinion that the only reason for the existence of Northern Securities was to create a monopoly on railroad traffic across the northern part of the country. The court ordered the company to be disbanded by selling the railroads it had acquired.

The minority of four Supreme Court justices felt that the government had gone too far in arguing that there was no difference between owning stock in a company and acting in a way to interfere with interstate commerce. Taken to its extreme, wrote Justice Oliver Wendell Holmes (1841–1935), the federal government could conceivably argue that any ownership of property might result in discouraging competition (referred to as restraint of trade) and therefore was a proper subject for regulation by the federal government.

The arguments put forth by both sides have remained a hot topic of political debate. The question of how much federal regulation is proper and good for people, and for business, is still an issue in the twenty-first century.

Things to remember while reading the excerpt from *Northern Securities Co.* v. *United States:*

- Supreme Court cases are often argued in terms that seem removed from the issue at hand. In the case of Northern Securities, one such argument was whether applying the Sherman Antitrust Act to a holding company (a company whose only purpose was to own stock, as opposed to operating a business) was something new, or just a continuation of well-established law. Both sides of the Supreme Court argued in their legal opinions that nothing new was (or should be) happening in this case. The majority argued that regulating Northern Securities by disallowing it was following well-established precedents (previous cases). The minority argued that regulating Northern Securities by disallowing it was violating well-established precedents. The argument was significant because the Supreme Court tries to determine, and follow, how similar disputes over the law have been decided in the past, since the court has no Constitutional power to create new laws.

- The growth of American railroads had been accompanied by many consolidations and sales of smaller companies to larger ones. Typically, a company would lay railroad track only between two cities. In a region, there might be many companies controlling small railroads that could not make money on their own. Consequently, larger companies would buy up smaller railroads to create a network of railroads that connected towns throughout a region. This practice had long been recognized as the nature of the business; did the Northern Securities Company do something beyond this sort of consolidation? The owners said no; the government said yes.

- The legal case of Northern Securities was also a political issue. President Roosevelt was labeled a progressive, a politician who believed the government needed to provide a counter-weight to the power of private businesses. Some of his political opponents argued that the government had no business interfering with business, and that in fact privately owned businesses were a necessary check on government power. This fundamental argument over the role of government and private property was carried out in the *Northern Securities* case in a slightly different form. The two sides argued over the relative powers of the federal government and the *state* governments (which were often sympathetic to big businesses to gain an advantage over other states in attracting jobs) to regulate corporations, and the issue of who owned stock in corporations.

- The Supreme Court in this case was deciding on whether a lower court was right in upholding the federal government's suit challenging the formation of the Northern Securities Company. For that reason, the majority opinion sometimes refers to the court's "affirmance," or upholding, of "the case below," meaning the ruling of the lower court.

- After the Supreme Court justices decided the case, they asked one justice, John Marshall Harlan (1833–1911), to write the Court's opinion, or finding. Occasionally, legal opinions use advanced vocabulary or refer to familiar things with unfamiliar words (or use familiar words to describe unfamiliar things). For example, this case uses the word "combinations" to refer to companies that own other companies.

Excerpt from NORTHERN SECURITIES COMPANY et al., **Appts.**, v. UNITED STATES

*Mr. Justice Harlan announced the **affirmance** of the **decree** of the **circuit court**, and delivered the following opinion: ...*

The Great Northern Railway Company and the Northern Pacific Railway Company owned, controlled, and operated separate lines of railway,—the former road [i.e., the Great Northern] extending from Superior, and from Duluth and St. Paul [Minnesota], to Everett, Seattle [Washington], and Portland [Oregon], with a branch line to Helena [Montana]; the latter [i.e., the Northern Pacific] extending from Ashland, and from Duluth and St. Paul [Minnesota], to Helena [Montana], Spokane, Seattle, Tacoma [Washington] and Portland [Oregon]. The two lines, main and branches, about 9,000 miles in length, were and are parallel and competing lines across the continent through the northern tier of states between the Great Lakes and the Pacific, and the two companies were engaged in active competition for freight and passenger traffic, each road connecting at its respective terminals with lines of railway, or with lake and river steamers, or with seagoing vessels.... Prior to November 13th, 1901, defendant [James J.] Hill and associate **stockholders** of the Great Northern Railway Company, and defendant [J. Pierpont] Morgan and associate stockholders of the Northern Pacific Railway Company, entered into a **combination** to form, under the laws of New Jersey, a **holding corporation**, to be called the Northern Securities Company....

Early in 1901 the Great Northern and Northern Pacific Railway Companies, having in view the **ultimate** placing of their two systems under a common control, united in the purchase of the capital stock of the Chicago, Burlington, & Quincy Railway Company, giving in payment, upon an agreed basis of exchange, the **joint bonds** of the Great Northern and Northern Pacific Railway Companies.... In this manner the two purchasing companies became the owners of ... the Chicago, Burlington, & Quincy Railway Company, whose lines **aggregated** about 8,000 miles, and extended from St. Paul [Minnesota] to Chicago, and from St. Paul and Chicago to Quincy, Burlington, Des Moines [Iowa], St. Louis, Kansas City, St.

Appts.: Appellants; group appealing a previous court ruling.

Affirmance: Agreement.

Decree: Ruling.

Circuit court: A Federal court below the Supreme Court, whose decisions can be appealed to the Supreme Court.

Stockholders: Persons owning shares of public companies.

Combination: Partnership.

Holding corporation: A company whose only purpose is to own other companies.

Ultimate: Final.

Joint bonds: Shares of two or more companies.

Aggregated: Totaled.

Justice John Marshall Harlan wrote the opinion of the Supreme Court in *Northern Securities Company* v. *United States*. *Reproduced by permission of the Library of Congress.*

Capital: Accumulated wealth.

Franchises: Groups.

Bill: Document.

Vesting: Putting.

To wit: Namely.

Inducement: Offer; incentive.

Virtual: Practical.

Joseph [Missouri], Omaha Lincoln [Nebraska], Denver [Colorado], Cheyenne [Wyoming], and Billings [Montana], where it connected with the Northern Pacific Railroad. By this purchase of stock the Great Northern and Northern Pacific acquired full control of the Chicago, Burlington, & Quincy main line and branches.

Prior to November 13th, 1901, defendant Hill and associate stockholders of the Great Northern Railway Company, and defendant Morgan and associate stockholders of the Northern Pacific Railway Company, entered into a combination to form, under the laws of New Jersey, a holding corporation, to be called the Northern Securities Company ... to which company, in exchange for its own capital stock upon a certain basis and at a certain rate, was to be turned over the capital stock, or a controlling interest in the **capital** stock, of each of the constituent railway companies, with power in the holding corporation to vote such stock and in all respects to act as the owner thereof, and to do whatever it might deem necessary in aid of such railway companies or to enhance the value of their stocks. In this manner the interests of individual stockholders in the property and **franchises** of the two independent and competing railway companies were to be converted into an interest in the property and franchises of the holding corporation. Thus, as stated in article 6 of the **bill**, "by making the stockholders of each system jointly interested in both systems, and by practically pooling the earnings of both for the benefit of the former stockholders of each, and by **vesting** the selection of the directors and officers of each system in a common body, **to wit**, the holding corporation, with not only the power, but the duty, to pursue a policy which would promote the interests, not of one system at the expense of the other, but of both at the expense of the public, all **inducement** for competition between the two systems was to be removed, a **virtual** consolidation effected, and a monopoly of the interstate and foreign commerce formerly carried on by the two systems as independent competitors established." ...

The government charges that if the combination was held not to be in violation of the [1890 Sherman Antitrust] act of Congress, then all efforts of the national government to preserve to the people the benefits of free competition among carriers engaged in **interstate commerce** will be **wholly unavailing**, and all transcontinental lines, indeed, the entire railway systems of the country, may be absorbed, merged, and consolidated, thus placing the public at the absolute mercy of the holding corporation....

In our judgment, the evidence fully sustains the **material allegations** of the **bill**, and shows a violation of the act of Congress, in so far as it declares illegal every combination or **conspiracy** in **restraint** of commerce among the several states and with foreign nations, and forbids attempts to monopolize such commerce or any part of it....

It is **indisputable** upon this record that under the leadership of the defendants Hill and Morgan the stockholders of the Great Northern and Northern Pacific Railway corporations, having competing and substantially parallel lines from the Great Lakes and the Mississippi river to the Pacific ocean at Puget Sound combined and conceived the scheme of organizing a corporation under the laws of New Jersey which should hold the shares of the stock of the constituent companies; such shareholders, **in lieu** of their shares in those companies, to receive, upon an agreed basis of value, shares in the holding corporation.... The stockholders of these two competing companies disappeared, as such, for the moment, but immediately reappeared as stockholders of the holding company, which was thereafter to guard the interests of both sets of stockholders as a unit, and to manage, or cause to be managed, both lines of railroad as if held in one ownership. Necessarily by this combination or arrangement the holding company in the fullest sense dominates the situation in the interest of those who were stockholders of the constituent companies; as much so, for every practical purpose, as if it had been itself a railroad corporation which had built, owned, and operated both lines for the exclusive benefit of its stockholders. Necessarily, also, the constituent companies ceased, under such a combination, to be in active competition for trade and commerce along their respective lines, and have become, practically, one powerful consolidated corporation, by the name of a holding corporation, the principal, if not the sole, object for the formation of which was to carry out the purpose of the original combination, under which competition between the constituent companies would cease. Those who

Interstate commerce: Business between two or more states.

Wholly unavailing: Completely futile.

Material allegations: Relevant charges, accusations.

Bill: Lawsuit.

Conspiracy: Secret plan.

Restraint: Restriction.

Indisputable: Without doubt.

In lieu: Instead.

were stockholders of the Great Northern and Northern Pacific and became stockholders in the holding company are now interested in preventing all competition between the two lines, and, as owners of stock or of certificates of stock in the holding company, they will see to it that no competition is tolerated.... No scheme or device could more certainly come within the words of the [Sherman Antitrust] act,—"combination in the form of a trust or otherwise ... in restraint of commerce among the several states or with foreign nations."...

The circuit court was undoubtedly right when it said—all the judges of that court **concurring**—that the combination referred to "led inevitably to the following results: First, it placed the control of the two roads in the hands of a single person, to wit, the Securities Company [corporations are a sort of artificial person, under the law], by virtue of its ownership of a large majority of the stock of both companies; second, it destroys every motive for competition between two roads engaged in interstate traffic, which were natural competition for business, by pooling the earnings of the two roads for the common benefit of the stockholders of both companies." ...

[Based on earlier Supreme Court decisions it is clear] that although the act of Congress known as the anti-trust act has no reference to the mere manufacture or production of articles or **commodities** within the limits of the several states, it does embrace and declare to be illegal every contract, combination, or conspiracy, in whatever form, of whatever nature, and whoever may be **parties to** it, which directly or necessarily operates in restraint of trade or commerce among the several states or with foreign nations;

That the act is not limited to restraints of interstate and international trade or commerce that are unreasonable in their nature, but embraces all direct restraints imposed by any combination, conspiracy, or monopoly upon such trade or commerce;

That railroad carriers engaged in interstate or international trade or commerce are **embraced** by the act;

That combinations, even among private manufacturers or dealers, whereby interstate or international commerce is restrained, are equally embraced by the act;

That Congress has the power to establish rules by which interstate and international commerce shall be governed, and, by the anti-trust act, has **prescribed** the rule of free competition among those engaged in such commerce;

Concurring: Agreeing.

Commodities: Goods.

Parties to: Involved in.

Embraced: Covered.

Prescribed: Ordered.

That every combination or conspiracy which would extinguish competition between otherwise competing railroads engaged in interstate trade or commerce, and which would in that way restrain such trade or commerce, is made illegal by the act;

That the natural effect of competition is to increase commerce, and an agreement whose direct effect is to prevent this play of competition restrains instead of promoting trade and commerce;

That to **vitiate** a combination such as the act of Congress condemns, it need not be shown that the combination, in fact, results or will result, in a total suppression of trade or in a complete monopoly, but it is only essential to show that, by its necessary operation, it tends to restrain interstate or international trade or commerce or tends to create a monopoly in such trade or commerce and to deprive the public of the advantages that flow from free competition;

That the constitutional **guaranty of liberty of contract** does not prevent Congress from prescribing the rule of free competition for those engaged in interstate and international commerce; and,

That under its power to regulate commerce among the several states and with foreign nations, Congress had authority to enact the statute in question....

The means employed in respect of the combinations forbidden by the anti-trust act, and which Congress deemed **germane** to the end to be accomplished, was to prescribe as a rule for interstate and international commerce (not for domestic commerce [within one state]) that it should not be **vexed** by combinations, conspiracies, or monopolies which restrain commerce by destroying or restricting competition. We say that Congress has prescribed such a rule, because, in all the prior cases in this court, the anti-trust act has been **construed** as forbidding any combination which, by its necessary operation, destroys or restricts free competition among those engaged in interstate commerce; in other words, that to destroy or restrict free competition in interstate commerce was to restrain such commerce. Now, can this court say that such a rule is prohibited by the Constitution or is not one that Congress could appropriately prescribe when exerting its power under the commerce clause of the Constitution [that gives the federal government the right to regulate business carried on between states]? Whether the free operation of the normal laws of competition is a wise and wholesome rule for trade and commerce is an economic question which this court need not consider or determine. Undoubtedly, there are those who

Vitiate: Make ineffective.

Guaranty of liberty of contract: Protection of contracts.

Germane: Relevant.

Vexed: Disturbed.

Construed: Understood.

think that the general business interests and **prosperity** of the country will be best promoted if the rule of competition is not applied. But there are others who believe that such a rule is more necessary in these days of enormous wealth than it ever was in any former period of our history. Be all this as it may, Congress has, in effect, recognized the rule of free competition by declaring illegal every combination or conspiracy in restraint of interstate and international commerce. As, in the judgment of Congress, the public convenience and the general welfare will be best **subserved** when the natural laws of competition are left undisturbed by those engaged in interstate commerce, and as Congress has **embodied** that rule in a statute, that must be, for all, the end of the matter, if this is to remain a government of laws, and not of men....

Indeed, when Congress declared contracts, combinations, and conspiracies in restraint of trade or commerce to be illegal, it did nothing more than apply to interstate commerce a rule that had been long applied by the several states when dealing with combinations that were in restraint of their domestic commerce. The decisions in state courts upon this general subject are not only numerous and instructive, but they show the circumstances under which the anti-trust act was passed. It may well be assumed that Congress, when enacting that statute, shared the general apprehension that a few powerful corporations or combinations sought to obtain, and, unless restrained, would obtain, such absolute control of the entire trade and commerce of the country as would be **detrimental** to the general welfare....

And all, we take it, will agree, as established firmly by the decisions of this court, that the power of Congress over commerce extends to all the **instrumentalities** of such commerce, and to every device that may be employed to interfere with the freedom of commerce among the states and with foreign nations. Equally, we assume, all will agree that the Constitution and the legal enactments of Congress are, by **express** words of the Constitution, the supreme law of the land, anything in the constitution and laws of any state to the contrary notwithstanding....

No state can, by merely creating a corporation, or in any other mode, project its authority into other states, and across the continent, so as to prevent Congress from exerting the power it possesses under the Constitution over interstate and international commerce, or so as to **exempt** its corporation engaged in interstate commerce from obedience to any rule lawfully established by Con-

Prosperity: Success.

Subserved: Served as a means of aiding.

Embodied: Incorporated.

Detrimental: Damaging.

Instrumentalities: Tools.

Express: Clearly stated.

Exempt: Free.

Industrial Revolution: Primary Sources

gress for such commerce. It cannot be said that any state may give a corporation, created under its laws, authority to restrain interstate or international commerce against the will of the nation as lawfully expressed by Congress. Every corporation created by a state is necessarily subject to the supreme law of the land....

The court may make any order necessary to bring about the **dissolution** or suppression of an illegal combination that restrains interstate commerce. All this can be done without **infringing** in any degree upon the just authority of the states. The affirmance of the judgment below will only mean that no combination, however powerful, is stronger than the law, or will be permitted to avail itself of the pretext that to prevent it doing that which, if done, would defeat a legal enactment of Congress, is to attack the reserved rights of the states....

We repeat that no state can **endow** any of its corporations, or any combination of its citizens, with authority to restrain interstate or international commerce, or to disobey the national will as manifested in legal enactments of Congress. So long as Congress keeps within the limits of its authority as defined by the Constitution, infringing no rights recognized or secured by that instrument, its regulations of interstate and international commerce, whether **founded** in wisdom or not, must be submitted to by all. Harm, and only harm, can come from the failure of the courts to recognize this fundamental principle of constitutional construction. To depart from it because of the circumstances of special cases, or because the rule, in its operation, may possibly affect the interests of business, is to endanger the safety and integrity of our institutions and make the Constitution mean not what it says, but what interested parties wish it to mean at a particular time and under particular circumstances. The supremacy of the law is the foundation rock upon which our institutions rest.

Dissolution: Breakup.

Infringing: Blocking.

Endow: Give.

Founded: Established.

What happened next ...

As a result of the Supreme Court decision, the Northern Securities Company was broken up. Hill and Morgan were not allowed to form a common company that owned two competing railroads.

Theodore Roosevelt thought his successor, William Howard Taft (pictured), was not aggressive enough in sustaining the Roosevelt policies of government regulation of corporations. *Reproduced by permission of the Library of Congress.*

In a much larger sense, the *Northern Securities* decision opened the way for greatly expanded regulation by the federal government of companies, most of which engage in interstate commerce. In effect, the court said that by granting the federal government the right to regulate interstate commerce, it also gave the federal government the right to regulate many other aspects of business that previously were state matters.

In a practical sense, this case (and others like it) defined the modern federal government, and its role in regulating many aspects of business, ranging from food safety to the operation of airlines and railroads.

The outcome of *Northern Securities* pleased President Theodore Roosevelt. But in 1912 Roosevelt became frustrated with the record of his successor, President William Howard Taft (1857–1930), partly on the grounds that Taft had not been as aggressive as Roosevelt would have liked in regulating corporate behavior. Consequently Roosevelt decided to challenge Taft for the Republican presidential nomination in 1912. Roosevelt lost and started his own party, the Progressive Party. But in the presidential election that year, the Republican vote was split between Taft and Roosevelt, and Democrat Woodrow Wilson (1856–1924) won the election. In some respects, the split of the Republicans was permanent, since in later years the Republican Party became associated with opposition to federal regulation and the Democrats were, more often than not, the champions of such regulation.

Did you know ...

Public sentiment against giant corporations that controlled whole industries started as early as 1880. It took over twenty years before the federal government, under President

Theodore Roosevelt, got around to challenging the "trusts" in court. Seven years after the *Northern Securities* case, an even larger trust was "busted" by the Supreme Court. It was the oil trust known as Standard Oil, owned by John D. Rockefeller (1839–1937), who was by then the richest person in the country.

For more information

Books

Gellhorn, Ernest, and William E. Kovacic. *Antitrust Law and Economics in a Nutshell.* 4th ed. St. Paul, MN: West Publishing Co., 1994.

Kovaleff, Theodore P., ed. *The Antitrust Impulse: An Economic, Historical, and Legal Analysis.* Armonk, NY: M. E. Sharpe, 1994.

Letwin, William. *Law and Economic Policy in America: The Evolution of the Sherman Antitrust Act.* New York: Random House, 1965.

Web Sites

"Northern Securities Co. v. United States, 193 U.S. 197 (1904). " *Cornell Law School.* http:// www2.law.cornell.edu (accessed on April 11, 2003).

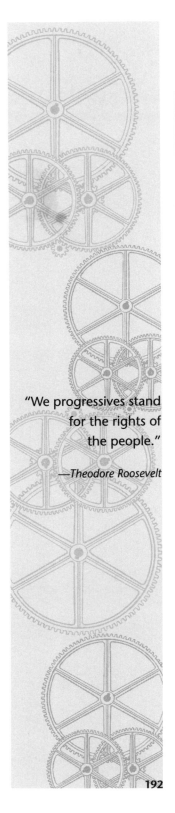

Progressive Party Documents

Excerpt from the Platform of the Progressive Party
*Excerpt from Address by Theodore Roosevelt before the
Convention of the National Progressive Party in Chicago*

August 6–7, 1912

In the summer of 1912, Theodore Roosevelt (1858–1919) was the most popular politician in America. As a Republican, he had been president for seven-and-a-half-years, from the assassination of William McKinley in September 1901 until March 1909. Near the end of his second term, he decided not to run for another term.

But Roosevelt was not happy with his Republican successor, William Howard Taft (1857–1930). The two disagreed particularly over the issue of conservation of natural resources. Both men were dedicated "trustbusters" who favored government lawsuits to break up large monopolies (companies exercising exclusive control of a particular area of commerce) in industries such as railroads and oil. Roosevelt also took a more aggressive approach to issues of social reform, such as child labor and minimum wages.

In February 1912 Roosevelt declared that he would again be a candidate for the presidency, challenging Taft for the Republican nomination. But President Taft influenced many Republican Party officials, and he defeated Roosevelt for the Republican nomination at the party's convention in

June 1912. Frustrated by the Republicans, Roosevelt declared that he was as fit as a bull moose, giving his campaign a symbol (the bull moose) of robust energy. Roosevelt's party was called the Progressive Party, but it was more often called by its nickname: the Bull Moose Party.

The Progressive Party was organized to address many of the social problems that had arisen from the rapid rise of factories where workers tended to machinery that did the work formerly done by hand. These problems included long hours and low pay, bad housing, and lack of education. They also included dishonest dealings in the stock market and bribery of public officials. The Progressive Party sought to pass government regulations to protect workers, regulate financial dealings, and prosecute corrupt public officials, as well as to tax the income of wealthy business owners. The term "progressive movement" represented the idea that government should actively address social problems.

Another approach to the social problems of industrialization was represented on the ballot in 1912 by the Socialist Party, led by Eugene Debs (1855–1926). The Socialists favored government ownership of big corporations, which would then be controlled democratically. The Socialists seemed too drastic for most voters in 1912, and Debs received just under one million votes, or about 6 percent of the total.

Things to remember while reading excerpts from the Progressive Party documents:

- A political party platform is a list of ideas and promises. It is written to appeal to as many voters as possible. Once a political party gets into office, some of the promises made in its platform may prove impossible (or inconvenient) to keep. Party platforms are useful, however, in understanding the principles and ideals that politicians believe will succeed in an election. Nevertheless, the 1912 platform of the Progressive Party is a good catalogue of social problems that grew from the Industrial Revolution in an era when government regulation was at a minimum.

- The argument over the relationship between the federal government and business has continued into the twenty-first century. In the early years of the Industrial Revolution, it was widely believed that the government had no active role to play in business. Consequently, companies were free to follow the policies they thought would benefit them most. As time went on, it became obvious that many of those policies—low wages and hiring children for dangerous work, for example—were resulting in widespread human suffering. The Progressive Party represented people who believed that business owners would never voluntarily correct these abuses, and that the only possible answer was government regulations to require that factories pay a minimum wage and laws preventing the hiring of children.

• Every political platform engages in a certain amount of simplification and exaggeration. For example, the Progressive platform accused the Republican Party of the "deliberate betrayal of its trust" by becoming too close to business interests. In fact, President Taft had been at least as aggressive as Theodore Roosevelt in attacking the trusts, or monopolies, by going to court to enforce laws prohibiting such activities. All political platforms and speeches need to be read with the understanding that politicians are trying to win votes, not necessarily to speak the pure truth.

• Similarly, just because an item is on a party's platform does not mean other parties oppose it. For example, the Progressive Party favored creating a U.S. Department of Labor to attend to the problems and issues of working people. In fact, President Taft signed a law creating the Department of Labor in March 1913, only days before he left office.

Excerpts from the Platform of the Progressive Party, August 7, 1912

The conscience of the people, in a time of grave national problems, has called into being a new party, born of the Nation's awakened sense of justice. We of the Progressive Party here dedicate ourselves to the fulfillment of the duty laid upon us by our fathers to maintain that gov-

ernment of the people, by the people and for the people [mentioned in the Declaration of Independence] whose foundation they laid.

We hold with Thomas Jefferson and Abraham Lincoln that the people are the masters of their Constitution, to fulfill its purposes and to safeguard it from those who, by **perversion** of its intent, would convert it into an instrument of injustice. In accordance with the needs of each generation the people must use their **sovereign** powers to establish and maintain equal opportunity and industrial justice, to secure which this Government was founded and without which no republic can endure.

This country belongs to the people who inhabit it. Its resources, its business, its institutions and its laws should be utilized, maintained or altered in whatever manner will best promote the general interest.

It is time to set the **public welfare** in the first place.

Progressive Party candidate Theodore Roosevelt.
Reproduced by permission of Getty Images.

The Old Parties

Political parties exist to secure responsible government and to execute the will of the people.

From these great tasks both of the **old parties** have turned aside. Instead of instruments to promote the general welfare, they have become the tools of corrupt interests which use them **impartially** to serve their selfish purposes. Behind the **ostensible** government sits enthroned an invisible government, owing no allegiance and acknowledging no responsibility to the people.

To destroy this invisible government, to dissolve the unholy alliance between corrupt business and corrupt politics is the first task of the statesmanship of the day.

The deliberate betrayal of its trust by the Republican Party, and the fatal incapacity of the Democratic Party to deal with the new issues of the new time, have compelled the people to forge a new instrument of government through which to give effect to their will in laws and institutions.

Perversion: Willful destruction.

Sovereign: Supreme.

Public welfare: Well-being.

Old parties: Republicans and Democrats.

Impartially: Without prejudice.

Ostensible: Outward appearance.

***Unhampered** by tradition, uncorrupted by power, undismayed by the magnitude of the task, the new party offers itself as the instrument of the people to sweep away old abuses, to build a new and nobler **commonwealth**....*

Nation and State

Up to the limit of the Constitution, and later by amendment of the Constitution, if found necessary, we advocate bringing under effective national jurisdiction those problems which have expanded beyond reach of the individual states.

*It is as **grotesque** as it is intolerable that the several States should by unequal laws in matters of common concern become competing commercial agencies, **barter** the lives of their children, the health of their women and the safety and well-being of their working people for the profit of their financial interests.*

The extreme insistence on States' rights by the Democratic Party in the Baltimore platform demonstrates anew its inability to understand the world into which it has survived or to administer the affairs of a Union of States which have in all essential respects become one people.

Social and Industrial Strength

The supreme duty of the Nation is the conservation of human resources through an enlightened measure of social and industrial justice. We pledge ourselves to work unceasingly in State and Nation for:—

*Effective legislation looking to the prevention of industrial accidents, occupational diseases, overwork, involuntary unemployment, and other **injurious** effects incident to modern industry;*

The fixing of minimum safety and health standards for the various occupations, and the exercise of the public authority of State and Nation, including the Federal control over inter-State commerce and the taxing power, to maintain such standards;

The prohibition of child labor;

Minimum wage standards for working women, to provide a living scale in all industrial occupations;

The prohibition of night work for women and the establishment of an eight hour day for women and young persons;

One day's rest in seven for all wage-workers;

Unhampered: Unrestrained.

Commonwealth: A political unit serving the greater good for the most people.

Grotesque: Ugly.

Barter: Exchange.

Injurious: Harmful.

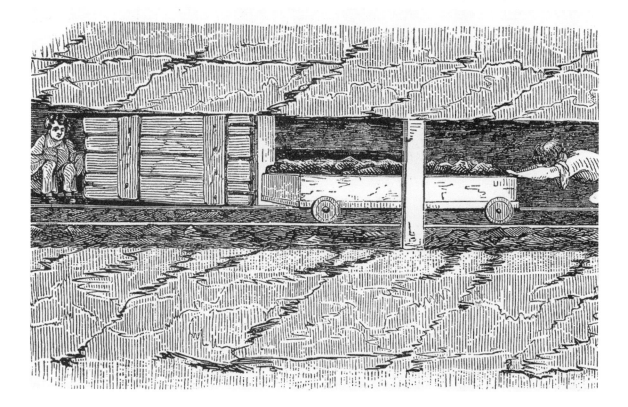

The abolition of the **convict contract labor system**; substituting a system of prison production for governmental consumption only; and the application of prisoners' earnings to the support of their dependent families;

Publicity as to wages, hours and conditions and labor; full reports upon industrial accidents and diseases, and the opening to public inspection of all **tallies**, weights, measures and check systems on labor products;

Standards of compensation for death by industrial accident and injury and trade diseases which will transfer the burden of lost earnings from the families of working people to the industry, and thus to the community;

The protection of home life against the hazards of sickness, irregular employment and old age through the adoption of a system of social insurance adapted to American use;

The development of the creative labor power of America by lifting the last load of **illiteracy** from American youth and establishing

This image depicts children working in a coal mine. Theodore Roosevelt called for the banishment of child labor in the Progressive Party platform of 1912. *Reproduced by permission of the Library of Congress.*

Convict contract labor system: Program in which prisoners were sent to factories and their wages paid to the state.

Tallies: Counts.

Illiteracy: Inability to read.

continuation schools for industrial education under public control and encouraging agricultural education and demonstration in rural schools;

The establishment of industrial research laboratories to put the methods and discoveries of science at the service of American producers.

We favor the organization of the workers, men and women as a means of protecting their interests and of promoting their progress.

Business

We believe that true popular government, justice and prosperity go hand in hand, and so believing, it is our purpose to secure that large measure of general prosperity which is the fruit of legitimate and honest business, **fostered** by equal justice and by sound progressive laws....

We therefore demand a strong National regulation of inter-State corporations. The corporation is an essential part of modern business. The concentration of modern business, in some degree, is both inevitable and necessary for National and international business efficiency, but the existing concentration of vast wealth under a corporate system, unguarded and uncontrolled by the Nation, has placed in the hands of a few men enormous, secret, irresponsible power over the daily life of the citizen—a power **insufferable** in a free government and certain of abuse.

This power has been abused, in **monopoly** of National resources, in **stock watering**, in unfair competition and unfair privileges, and finally in **sinister** influences on the public agencies of State and Nation. We do not fear commercial power, but we insist that it shall be exercised openly, under publicity, supervision and regulation of the most efficient sort, which will preserve its good while **eradicating** and preventing its evils.

To that end we urge the establishment of a strong Federal administrative commission of high standing, which shall maintain permanent active supervision over industrial corporations....

Equal **Suffrage**

The Progressive Party, believing that no people can justly claim to be a true democracy which denies political rights on account of sex, pledges itself to the task of securing equal suffrage to men and women alike....

Fostered: Supported.

Insufferable: Unbearable.

Monopoly: Complete control.

Stock watering: Manipulation of the market.

Sinister: Evil.

Eradicating: Wiping out.

Suffrage: Right to vote.

Department of Labor

*We pledge our party to establish a Department of Labor with a seat in the **cabinet**, and with wide jurisdiction over matters affecting the conditions of labor and living....*

Health

We favor the union of all the existing agencies of the Federal Government dealing with the public health into a single National health service....

Patents

*We pledge ourselves to the enactment of a **patent law** which will make it impossible for patents to be suppressed or used against the public welfare in the interests of injurious monopolies.*

Inter-State Commerce Commission

We pledge our party to secure to the Inter-State Commerce Commission the power to value the physical property of railroads. In order that the power of the commission to protect the people may not be impaired or destroyed, we demand the abolition of the Commerce Court.

Good Roads

*We recognize the vital importance of good roads and we pledge our party to foster their extension in every proper way, and we favor the early construction of National highways. We also favor the extension of the **rural free delivery service**....*

*We favor the **ratification** of the pending amendment to the Constitution giving the Government power to **levy** an income tax....*

The Immigrant

*Through the establishment of industrial standards we propose to secure to the **able-bodied** immigrant and to his native fellow workers a larger share of American opportunity.*

*We denounce the fatal policy of indifference and neglect which has left our enormous immigrant population to become the prey of chance and **cupidity**.*

*We favor governmental action to encourage the distribution of immigrants away from the congested cities, to rigidly supervise all private agencies dealing with them and to promote their **assimilation**, education and advancement....*

Cabinet: Advisers to the president of the United States.

Patent law: Exclusive right to earn money from an invention.

Rural free delivery service: Mail to farmers.

Ratification: Approved.

Levy: Impose.

Able-bodied: Capable.

Cupidity: Excessive desire.

Assimilation: Inclusion into society.

Government Business Organization

We pledge our party to readjustment of the business methods of the National Government and a proper co-ordination of the Federal bureaus, which will increase the economy and efficiency of the Government service, prevent duplications and secure better results to the taxpayers for every dollar expended.

Government Supervision Over Investment

*The people of the United States are **swindled** out of many millions of dollars every year, through worthless investments. The plain people, the wage-earner and the men and women with small savings, have no way of knowing the merit of concerns sending out highly colored **prospectuses** offering stock for sale, prospectuses that make big returns seem certain and fortunes easily within grasp.*

We hold it to be the duty of the Government to protect its people from this kind of piracy. We, therefore, demand wise carefully-thought-out legislation that will give us such Governmental supervision over this matter as will furnish to the people of the United States this much-needed protection, and we pledge ourselves thereto.

Conclusion

*On these principles and on the recognized desirability of uniting the Progressive forces of the Nation into an organization which shall **unequivocally** represent the Progressive spirit and policy we appeal for the support of all American citizens without regard to previous political **affiliations**.*

Excerpt from Address by Theodore Roosevelt before the Convention of the National Progressive Party in Chicago, August 6, 1912

*We Progressives stand for the rights of the people. When these rights can best be secured by insistence upon States's rights, then we are for States's rights; when they can best be secured by insistence upon National rights, then we are for National rights. Interstate commerce can be effectively controlled only by the Nation. The States cannot control it under the Constitution, and to amend the Constitution by giving them control of it would amount to a **dissolution** of the Government. The worst of the big trusts have always **endeavored** to keep alive the feeling in favor of having the States themselves, and not the Nation, attempt to do this work, because they know that in the long run such effort would be ineffective.*

Swindled: Cheated.

Prospectuses: Pamphlets.

Unequivocally: Without compromise.

Affiliations: Connections.

Dissolution: Breaking apart.

Endeavored: Tried, attempted.

There is no surer way to prevent all successful effort to deal with the trusts than to insist that they be dealt with in the States rather than by the Nation, or to create a conflict between the States and the Nation on the subject. The well-meaning ignorant man who advances such a proposition does as much damage as if he were hired by the trusts themselves, for he is playing the game of every big crooked corporation in the country. The only effective way in which to regulate the trusts is through the exercise of the **collective** power

Theodore Roosevelt is depicted inspecting a bull moose, the mascot of the Progressive Party.
Reproduced by permission of the Library of Congress.

Collective: United.

of our people as a whole through the Governmental agencies established by the Constitution for this very purpose.

*Grave injustice is done by the Congress when it fails to give the National Government complete power in this matter; and still graver injustice by the Federal courts when they endeavor in any way to **pare down** the right of the people collectively to act in this matter as they deem wise; such conduct does itself tend to cause the creation of a twilight zone in which neither the Nation nor the States have power....*

*The **antitrust law** should be kept on the statute books and strengthened so as to make it genuinely and thoroughly effective against every big concern tending to monopoly or guilty of anti-social practices.*

At the same time, a National industrial commission should be created which should have complete power to regulate and control all the great industrial concerns engaged in inter-State business—which practically means all of them in this country....

*This commission should deal with all the abuses of the trust,—all the abuses such as those developed by the Government suit against the Standard Oil and Tobacco Trusts—as the Inter-State Commerce Commission now deals with rebates. It should have complete power to make the **capitalization** absolutely honest and put a stop to all stock watering. Such supervision over the issuance of corporate securities would put a stop to exploitation of the people by dishonest capitalists desiring to declare **dividends** on **watered securities**, and would open this kind of industrial property to ownership of the people at large. It should have free access to the books of each corporation and power to find out exactly how it treats its employees, its rivals, and the general public. It should have power to compel the unsparing publicity of all the acts of any corporation which goes wrong....*

Pare down: Reduce.

Antitrust law: A law that prohibits companies from avoiding competition by acquiring a monopoly on a particular industry.

Capitalization: Profit.

Dividends: Payments.

Watered securities: Unequal shares.

What happened next ...

Roosevelt and Taft split the Republican vote, with Roosevelt receiving 27.4 percent of the popular vote to Taft's 23.2 percent. But the Democrat, Woodrow Wilson, received

41.8 percent of the popular vote and won the election with 435 electoral votes.

In 1916 Theodore Roosevelt decided not to run again and the Progressive Party dissolved. But the ideas behind his candidacy did not disappear. Twelve years later, Senator Robert La Follette Sr. of Wisconsin ran unsuccessfully for the presidency as an independent who was supported by many progressives. In 1934 his son Robert La Follette Jr. formed a Progressive Party in Wisconsin and achieved some success in the state. In 1948 Henry Wallace organized a new Progressive Party to run for the White House against Harry Truman.

In the meantime, many if not most of the policies advocated by Roosevelt and the Progressive Party in 1912 eventually became law. Women achieved the vote in 1919, minimum wage laws were enacted, and bans on child labor eventually eliminated many of the wretched social conditions created by the Industrial Revolution.

Did you know . . .

Just eight months before the election of 1912, a dramatic strike by textile workers in Lawrence, Massachusetts, had brought the problems of workers to national attention. The strike, which included violent confrontations between strikers and state police and militiamen, involved many young women and girls employed in the many textile mills in Lawrence. Congressional hearings in March 1912 (see Camella Teoli entry) had made public the stories of these girls, among whom were many immigrants. The widespread national publicity, including photos showing militiamen (similar to members of today's National Guard) pointing rifles with bayonets at the strikers, brought widespread sympathy for the strikers.

For more information

Books

Duncan-Clark, S. J. *The Progressive Movement: Its Principles and Its Programme* (includes Platform of the Progressive Party). Boston: Small, Maynard & Co., 1913.

Gable, John A. *The Bull Moose Years: Theodore Roosevelt and the Progressive Party.* Port Washington, NY: Kennikat Press, 1978.

Howland, Harold. *Theodore Roosevelt and His Times: A Chronicle of the Progressive Movement* (includes the Address by Theodore Roosevelt). New Haven, CT: Yale University Press, 1921.

Kennedy, David M., ed. *Progressivism: The Critical Issues.* Boston: Little, Brown, 1971.

Pinchot, Amos. *History of the Progressive Party, 1912–1916.* New York: New York University Press, 1958.

Index

References to photos are
marked by (ill.); **bold** type
indicates primary source
entries and their page
numbers.

F

Fabian society 149
Factory Act of 1833 110
The Factory Girl's Last Day 106
Factory system 16 (ill.), 165 (ill.).
    See also Manufacturing
    agriculture and 137–138
    children and 13, 18, 54–55,
        58, 68–69, 99, 101–110, 114,
        117, 119, 120–122, 164–175,
        177, 203
    cigar making and 112–122
    competition and 56, 59–61
    cottage industries and 23, 102
    dangers of 11–12, 99, 156–163,
        164, 170–172, 177, 196, 197
    government regulation and
        101–102, 106, 158, 162–163,
        177
    hours and 29, 55, 99, 101–102,
        103–110, 117, 118, 177
    housing and 112–122,
        152–153
    immigration and 166
    labor and 1, 2, 13–19, 28–31,
        54–59, 61–62, 63–74,
        99–110, 112–122
    labor unions and 19, 100, 163
    meat processing and 135–145
    muckrakers and 135–145, 158
    productivity and 13–14, 19,
        54–61, 63
    property and 23, 25–28
    specialization in 3–11
    textiles and 54–62, 63–74, 102,
        156–163, 164–175, 203
    urbanization and 23
    violence and 104, 108, 109
    wages and 18, 19, 29–31, 64,
        117, 118, 168, 169, 172, 177
    wealth and 1, 2, 14, 15
    women and 18, 29
    work and 13–19, 28–29,
        103–109, 114–120, 136,
        138–139, 140–141, 145,
        168–174
Farming. *See* Agriculture
Fair Labor Standards Act 122
Fillmore, Millard 82–83
Finance. *See also* Business
    regulation of 200, 202

telegraph and 76, 77, 78,
    82–83, 84
Food 135–145, 141 (ill.). *See also*
    Agriculture
Food and Drug Act of 1906
    144–145
Frame Breaking Act 73
French Revolution 66

G

Gamble, Mr. 95
Germinal 123–134
Gompers, Samuel 100, **112–120,**
    113 (ill.), 122
Government. *See also* Govern-
    ment regulation; Politics;
    specific governmental bodies
    corruption in 113, 115
    finance and 76, 77, 78, 82–83
    labor and 62, 166, 167, 203
    reform of 14, 200
    social work and 153, 154
    telegraph and 76, 77, 78,
        82–83
Government regulation. See also
    specific governmental bodies;
    specific laws
    children and 106, 122, 164, 177
    factory system and 101–102,
        106, 158, 162–163, 177
    food processing and 136–137,
        144–145
    hours and 165, 167, 177,
        196–197
    monopolies and 97, 137,
        177–178, 179–191, 192, 194,
        200–202
    patents and 199
    social reform and 192–203
    taxes and 35, 43, 199
    Theodore Roosevelt and 158,
        177–178, 182, 190
    wages and 106, 122, 177,
        196–197
Grace, William 115
Great Northern Railroad 87, 179,
    183–186
Guizot, François 24

R

S